D0528684

EXAMINING NEWSPAPERS

The SAGE CommText Series

Series Editor:
EVERETTE E. DENNIS
Gannett Center for Media Studies, Columbia University

Founding Editor: F. GERALD KLINE, *late of the School of Journalism and Mass Communication, University of Minnesota*
Founding Associate Editor: SUSAN H. EVANS, *Annenberg School of Communications, University of Southern California*

The **SAGE CommText** series brings the substance of mass communication scholarship to student audiences by blending syntheses of current research with applied ideas in concise, moderately priced volumes. Designed for use both as supplementary readings and as "modules" with which the teacher can "create" a new text, the **SAGE CommTexts** give students a conceptual map of the field of communication and media research. Some books examine topical areas and issues; others discuss the implications of particular media; still others treat methods and tools used by communication scholars. Written by leading researchers with the student in mind, the **SAGE CommTexts** provide teachers in communication and journalism with solid supplementary materials.

Available in this series:

additional titles in preparation

Gerald Stone

EXAMINING NEWSPAPERS

What Research Reveals About America's Newspapers

Volume 20. The Sage COMMTEXT Series

SAGE PUBLICATIONS
The Publishers of Professional Social Science
Newbury Park   Beverly Hills   London   New Delhi

For information address:

SAGE Publications, Inc.
2111 West Hillcrest Drive
Newbury Park, California 91320

SAGE Publications Inc.
275 South Beverly Drive
Beverly Hills
California 90212

SAGE Publications Ltd.
28 Banner Street
London EC1Y 8QE
England

SAGE PUBLICATIONS India Pvt. Ltd.
M-32 Market
Greater Kailash I
New Delhi 110 048 India

Printed in the United States of America

Library of Congress Cataloging-in-Publication Data

Stone, Gerald C.
    Examining newspapers.

    (The Sage commtext series ; v. 20)
    Bibliography: p.
    Includes index.
    1. American newspapers. I. Title. II. Series.
PN4867.S76 1987   071'.3   87-13195
ISBN 0-8039-2952-8
ISBN 0-8039-2953-6 (pbk.)

CONTENTS

*This book is dedicated to
Leonard and Adele Stone,
loving parents.*

ACKNOWLEDGMENTS

My thanks to: Dr. Maxwell E. McCombs, Jesse H. Jones Centennial Professor in Communication and chairman of the Department of Journalism at the University of Texas at Austin, who served as mentor during my doctoral work at Syracuse University; to the late Dr. Elden Rawlings, who had faith in my idea to publish a journal of practical research for the newspaper industry; and to my friends and colleagues who have supported *Newspaper Research Journal* since its inception. Other colleagues who have worked with me as coauthors and have kept my interest in newspaper research alive include: Dan Garvey, Elinor Grusin, Barbara Hartung, Richard Lindeborg, Will Norton, John Schweitzer, Mike Stein, Wayne Towers, Edgar Trotter, Sandra Utt, David Weaver, Roger Wetherington, John Windhauser, Dwight Jensen, and a host of excellent students. My special thanks to Donna B. Stone, a patient and fair editor, and best friend; and to Dr. Everette E. Dennis, editor of the SAGE CommText Series.

INTRODUCTION

Without the benefit of research, the presses would still turn and the newspaper still publish. But what lands on the reader's front porch is all the better for research of the quality available today. This book furnishes a useful guide to current research.

Given the pace of life on a newspaper, making decisions on the basis of gut instinct is faster, certainly. And research often frustrates us by only confirming what already can be guessed. Of course that can be useful as well. What research provides is invaluable for moving decisions with big price tags off dead center and for generating a consensus among people—colleagues or customers—with diverse opinions. I can think of no area of newspapers that cannot benefit from the combination of competent research and intelligent application of the findings.

With the current and growing fragmentation of the media, particularly television, with more than 4 of 10 American homes already hooked up to cable, with more than one-third of all American households having videocassette recorders, with 11,000 different magazine titles being published in the United States, newspapers hunger for what research can tell them about being relevant to their audience and about competing successfully for people's time and dollars. We want to know who our readers are, and who they are not, what they like and do not like about us, what they rely on us for, how and when and where they read the paper, and how they use and regard newspapers compared to other media. We want to know whether we are using news space effectively: Should we change the mix of local, national, international, sports, and business news? Does anybody read the bridge column? Do they prefer our comics section or The Other Paper's? Would readers be interested in a weekly science section? In the hands of savvy editors, information of this sort can reinvigorate a newspaper and help them reach new audiences.

Although it is beyond the scope of Professor Stone's book, it is worth mentioning that these same sorts of research techniques have an even more direct bearing on content when the newsroom uses them to add substance and support to articles about problems, trends, or attitudes that would otherwise be difficult to quantify. For example, postelection polling in November 1986 revealed that race played an important role in the overwhelming defeat of Republican William Lucas's campaign to become Michigan's first black governor. Research also provided the backbone for two *Free Press* series examining the city of Detroit's image problem—one showing how the rest of the county views Detroit, one telling Detroiters how they view themselves.

Research plays a key role in other areas of the newspaper as well. Some examples:

Advertising—Research allows our sales representatives to show advertisers how their customer profile matches that of our readers as well as that of the readers and viewers of competing media.

Circulation—We learned what types of circulation discount offers were most effective and how long we were likely to retain a customer who signs up for a discounted subscription.

Production—We evaluated the impact on circulation of giving out-of-state customers papers with later news and sports, yet delivered at the accustomed time.

As the first chapter indicates, much of newspaper research is proprietary since it has been funded by individual newspapers or newspaper groups for the purpose of enhancing their own viability. Neveretheless as someone who has initiated and read the results of a considerable number of such research projects, I can tell you that what you will read in this book about the highlights of recent research on newspaper content and reader habits echoes generally much of what you might read in private research keyed to a specific city or publication. For that reason, this book will be a handy compendium for the editor who wants to gauge quickly whether any research exists to support an impending decision. Another section newspaper practitioners will find interesting and useful is the information about newsroom demographics.

For students, the sections on how newsrooms are organized and how content decisions are made can provide starting places, at least, for learning more about newspapers, although I caution against accepting any generalizations about newsrooms. They are all so very different. Newspapers' individuality and lack of conformity are, after all, part of why they are fascinating to study as well as to read.

> *—David Lawrence, Jr.*
> Publisher, Detroit *Free Press*

USING THE TEXT

Of course the subtitle is an exaggeration. No single volume could begin to contain the totality "What Research Reveals About America's Newspapers." A better subtitle might be "Some Findings from Some Research Studies on Some Topics Related to Newspapers." And the addendum might be "As Selected, Synthesized, and Interpreted by One Writer in the Mid-1980s." However, the square inches of book covers have limitations similar to those inflicted by the number of pages between the covers. Readers will recognize these limitations as the author openly admits them.

Still, the book is an attempt to present part of the body of knowledge gained over the years about newspapers and the newspaper industry. It is intended for students of journalism and communication as well as industry practitioners who might find the book useful as a single source covering a variety of topics—all related to how newspapers gather, write, edit, and disseminate information and how readers use newspapers. For instance, the author receives inquiries from industry practitioners nearly every month that go something like this: "I've been asked to speak at an international convention about trends in newspaper page design and the use of pictures. Where can I find some research on that topic? The speech is next week."

Three things are obvious: The speaker is already a recognized industry authority on design and photos, so the speech will go well regardless of whether it includes an overview of research on the topic; the speaker doesn't know a source from which to begin gathering research findings on his or her own field of expertise; and there's little hope of making the deadline. This text could help that speaker prepare his or her remarks—at least the next time such a speech is requested.

On the other hand, a recent inquiry was "I'm supposed to speak on newspaper special sections next week. Do you know of any research on special topic supplements or special sections newspapers occasionally publish?" Here the industry professional will get little assistance because the topic is not included in this text. Although special issues certainly deserve some research attention, they haven't been a popular research topic to date. Space limitations have resulted in many such omissions, a regrettable but necessary outcome of any selection process.

A primary audience for this text is the student who seeks a broad overview of the newspaper research field. This reader will find limitations as well, but should gain substantial insight about the major themes of research on the newspaper industry and some outcomes of investigations on those themes. References at the end of each chapter will lead a student to further readings on a specific interest.

Newspaper practitioners—those who are yet to be invited to deliver major presentations on their field of expertise—should also find this text useful. As a compilation, it is a single source with abundant information arranged in industry specialty areas: Reporters can learn what the research has provided about sources and writing a news article; editors can learn about broad categories of newspaper content and how audiences use the information newspapers provide.

The text also serves as a compendium of newspaper research findings for industry and academic researchers—a starting point from which to launch their own investigations.

In all, then, this text is intended as a map of newspaper research. To the extent it serves that purpose, it has reached its goal. As a synthesis of newspaper research, an effort has been made to provide outcomes substantiated by the bulk of findings on a range of topics. From those whose research has centered on the more controversial topics (Are newspaper groups a blessing or an evil?), the author asks temperance on the interpretations he has drawn. From those whose worthy research has been inadvertently omitted, the author asks understanding. It is an oversight.

> —*Gerald C. Stone*
> Memphis, Tennessee

1

WHAT HAS BEEN WRITTEN AND WHY

Research on newspapers mirrors the lengthy development of inquiry into the mass communication process generally with the exception that it focuses on a competitive industry involved in news and information dissemination.

In a profit-making industry much work is initiated, carried out, and reported under highly competitive conditions; hence much of it is never reported at all. Newspapers are born and exist in continual competitiveness. They compete against other papers—both daily and weekly papers, paid and freely circulated—mail circulars, magazines, billboards, the broadcast media, and cable. Continued survival often demands a cloak of secrecy about every tidbit of information regarding the newspaper's position in its market. Right or wrong, most individual newspapers and groups have subscribed to this view of fierce competition. Consequently, individual newspapers have retained a competitive edge that has kept them healthy, or at least alive. However, more evident today is the restricted growth of a body of knowledge about the newspaper industry (Hynds, 1975).

PROPRIETARY VERSUS PUBLIC RESEARCH

Two major types of research deal with the newspaper industry: (1) "public" research by newspaper organizations and independent scholars and (2) "proprietary" research by individual newspapers and the firms they hire. Studies in the former group are often fragmented. They follow the researchers' special interests or timely fads (Stamm, 1985; American Society of Newspaper Editors, 1985). The extent and quality of the latter group are a matter of speculation since the material simply is not available for perusal, although there has been some recent insight offered through computer banks of proprietary research (Einsiedel, 1983; see also Mohn, 1982).

Proprietary research has been extensive and perhaps more edifying (at least to industry practitioners who order it) than public research since it is more lavishly funded and often continuing. Commercial research firms contracted by individual newspapers often do major update studies of the local market annually. Some of these firms are Belden Associates; Market Opinion Research; Clarke, Matire & Bartolomeo; and MORI Research. Additionally, large newspaper groups, such as Gannett, Knight-Ridder, Times-Mirror, and Media General, conduct extensive proprietary research programs throughout the year. Occasionally the methodological approaches used are shared openly at meetings of the Newspaper Research Council. More often, both the research approaches and the results remain part of the private domain of the funding organization. An inkling of the extent of this proprietary research is suggested by the kinds of known studies.

(1) a massive computer bank of new themes compiled through a sophisti-
    cated, daily content analysis of a major metropolitan paper to enable
    prediction of what kinds of automobiles purchasers would want five
    years later
(2) a factor-analysis project that determined the relative importance of some
    dozen elements responsible for street sales of a major daily (Meyer, 1980)
(3) use of the Lusher Color Test to determine how people of different
    personalities select among newspapers
(4) identification of life-style types that contribute to readership patterns
    (Bryant, 1976)
(5) annual lists of averaged financial statement information on daily news-
    papers by circulation categories (Inland Press Association)

These are only some of the innovative approaches that have come to light, usually long after being developed by the private firms. Most of these research approaches are still not available for public scrutiny.

Fortunately, what is available for study does provide a substantial and valuable body of knowledge about newspapers. It includes: (1) cooperative research by organizations such as the Newspaper Advertising Bureau (NAB), the American Newspaper Publishers Association (ANPA), and others; (2) academic research available in scholarly publications such as *Journalism Quarterly, Newspaper Research Journal*, and others; (3) books and reports by both academic and industry scholars; and (4) special investigations funded by newspaper groups and foundations that receive attention in industry periodicals.

WHY NEWSPAPERS?

In spite of the newspaper industry's competitive nature, there is a surprisingly rich field of available research on this mass medium. Actually, relatively sophisticated research reports on the industry can be found prior to 1920 (Rogers, 1918). Using even the early 1950s as a starting point provides enough history of research on the newspaper industry in the United States.

Newspapers have been the focus of mass media research for a variety of reasons. Among them are the following: (1) They were the single dominant news medium for much of the twentieth century; (2) their content was easily accessed for study purposes, as opposed to the content of the film and broadcast media; (3) the professional background of mass media scholars during most of the twentieth century was more likely to have been in newspapering; (4) journalism schools were dominated by newspaper curricula through the 1960s; (5) the industry had funds for market research; and (6) there was more organization in the newspaper industry, which had developed a variety of press associations and newspaper groups capable of pooling funds for some research purposes.

Of these reasons, the binding thread is the newspaper industry's long domination of the mass field. Early editions of *Journalism Quarterly*, mass media's earliest continuing scholarly journal, confirm an overwhelming representation of topics related to newspapers.

Newspapers have possibly the widest variety of research needs among the mass media. Publishing a newspaper requires knowledge about information gathering, writing and editing news and opinion, graphics and design, advertising sales and design, circulation promotion, newsroom management, employee relations, printing, technological developments, distribution, maintaining market share, and, most importantly, audience effects. This industry's range of research needs is equivalent to that of the manufacture and sale of durable goods and one of the nation's major social institutions combined.

PATTERNS OF
SCHOLARLY RESEARCH THEMES

Newspaper research is in an infancy stage compared with other social sciences. While studying newspapers follows the general pattern of other social science research, it is compressed into fewer decades.

The earliest studies were press criticism, a tradition of research through essays on one or more aspects of the field. The tradition continues (Crouse, 1973). In the late 1800s and early 1900s, writing appeared to follow the "great man" style of historic study. This is still a popular approach (Halberstam, 1979). However, newsaper research was quick to apply more scientific social research tools and techniques. Even as it was being brought to its contemporary sophistication, newspaper research experimented with statistics and survey methods (Schramm, 1963). In fact, newspaper research used content analysis as a staple very early in its history (Berelson, 1952).

The patterns of scholarly research themes on newspapers follow the general outline of:

(1) What is right or wrong about how the newspaper industry operates; particularly is the content of newspapers serving the public?
(2) Which are the important newspapers and who are (or were) the key figures guiding them?
(3) How are the various departments of newspapers managed?
(4) How are news articles produced?
(5) What happens in the newspaper's internal selection process and what effect does that process have on the content of papers?
(6) What major news topics are covered in newspapers?
(7) Who does and does not read newspapers?
(8) Can principles be found that will provide the optimum quality, circulation, or income for newspapers?
(9) What is the newspaper's market position relative to other mass media?
(10) What effect does newspaper content have on audiences?
(11) Are there broad principles that explain individuals' or audiences' involvement with newspapers?

These themes overlap considerably. The list is not a distinct chronological presentation, although an attempt has been made to place the themes on a time continuum. Sadly, some of the more widely researched themes are not necessarily the most important, and the outcomes of several are no longer valid due to changes within the industry or society. Finally, some themes have been researched without great success. For example, while the audience for newspapers has been explicitly identified, for most practical purposes, the few attempts to derive broad principles about how audiences interact with the media have been disappointing.

One of the goals of this overview of research about newspapers is to discriminate between *knowledge* and *speculation*. In this case, *knowledge* is based on substantial research undertakings (or several lesser studies that together derive the same results), rigorously controlled and completed under conditions that may be assumed still to prevail. For instance, even a major study of how people rely on newspapers for public affairs information should be viewed with skepticism if completed before the advent of television in the early 1950s.

Speculation, on the other hand, is information that has been poorly or inconsistently supported. The topic may not have received much attention, the studies completed may have been too limited in scope to allow inferences, or there may be conflicting outcomes on the topic. In such cases, the weaknesses will be noted and the information will be identified as speculative. However, a speculative outcome may in fact be valid while an outcome identified as knowledge may be wrong. Such is the province of social science research.

HELP FROM THE OUTSIDE

Two developments in the past 60 years have benefited newspaper research, although neither was prompted by the newspaper industry. They are (1) scholars in numerous other disciplines realized understanding their own interest area was dependent on knowing more about the mass media; and (2) advances in research tools and techniques allowed the newspaper industry to grapple with increasingly complex problems. Although there is some overlap between the two, a brief, separate synopsis of these lending hands is worthwhile.

Associated Disciplines

As society evolved to an ever more complex social system, the mass media served as the gel that maintained the system. This seemingly theoretical statement is instead an extremely practical and functional truism that was condoned by the country's founding fathers and has been recognized with varying degrees of grudging acquiescence since. By World War I, it was evident that communicating with America's widely dispersed and heterogeneous population could be done only—but could be done effectively—through the mass media, chiefly newspapers at that time.

Those in the newspaper industry were becoming aware in the early 1900s that science, including the social sciences, was a topic suitable for continuing news stories: that psychology might explain why heinous crimes are committed or mathematics might provide new principles about light and energy (Bogart, 1968). Concurrently, it was increasingly apparent that people learned of events, discoveries, and new ways to view their environment primarily through their daily newspapers.

Political science, the discipline most likely to include newspapers as a key variable in its own research, was the first to do so. The Erie County study of what influenced a voter's decision about candidates in the 1940 presidential election remains a most impressive study of mass media effects (Lazarsfeld, Berelson, & Gaudet, 1944). While the Erie County study may be viewed as rudimentary today, in light of advances in both research methods and theory during the past 40 years, it nonetheless was a fortuitous project that brought attention to the mass media as a discipline worth investigation. The three political scientists who questioned Erie County voters about the mass media in effect founded mass communication research.

Sociology has provided significant input to the study of mass media and newspapers. Mass media are most frequently viewed as influencing large groups of people. Hence, a synergism has existed between sociologists—Robert E. Park and Morris Janowitz, for instance—and newspaper researchers in the study of both which groups use newspapers and how those groups are affected by newspapers (Bressler, 1968). A similar synergism has existed between newspaper research and psychology—Carl Hovland and Leon Festinger, for instance—since newspaper use actually takes place at the individual level (Blumler & Katz, 1974). Other disciplines contributing extensively to newspaper research include law, speech, English or writing, business administration, marketing and advertising, history, geography, library science, criminology, statistics, education, and economics. Some of these disciplines have had only minor impact while others, as in the Erie County study example, have found their researchers identified more with mass media or newspaper research than with the fields they originally studied (Schramm, 1963). The outcome for newspaper research has been considerable enrichment from cross-pollination by other disciplines. Instead of relying on a single perspective for study, newspaper research has dozens of successful grafts from other fields by scientists who found close association between what they had been trained to study and the mass media. No doubt many other disciplines can point to a richness they've gained from borrowed ideas, but it is unlikely another discipline can claim the same level of fertility that newspaper research received.

Research Techniques

Newspaper research gained momentum from developing research techniques, including advances in research methods and statistics.

Newspapers were doing some forms of advertising and readership research in the early 1900s. The early efforts were primitive, but that they were undertaken at all is tribute to an interest in measuring the newspaper's acceptance in its market.

Studies were along the line of Starch surveys of magazine advertising. Newsboys or ad sales persons took copies of the previous day's paper to subscriber homes and asked readers to mark what they had seen in the paper. The objective was to use the figures on ad readership to convince advertisers to purchase more space. However, an unanticipated benefit was knowledge gained about how people read a newspaper: what they look at on the page, how much of a story is read, how the eye follows page layouts, how the reader skips through the newspaper, and so forth. These studies unearthed findings about the importance of pictures and cutlines, large and clearly written headlines, the inverted-pyramid news writing style, and diagonal design patterns (Baskette & Sissors, 1977). But the early studies were based on a convenience sample, lack of rigor in interviewing techniques, little effort to ascertain reliability, and a host of other omissions and commissions likely to occur from an effort designed primarily to boost ad sales. Still, newspaper managers were among the first to realize their product and marketing effort could be improved through audience-feedback activities.

Note that the history and development of mass media research is, as yet, not well documented. Definitive investigations are currently under way to chart that history (Dennis, 1986). Until that work is complete, the following rough approximation is offered.

While scholarly research to about 1920 was primarily essays or critical commentary about newspapers, and case studies—the same approaches most other social sciences were using—newspaper researchers were aware of advances in statistical measurement and survey methodology (Emery, 1982). The earliest documented poll by a newspaper was in 1824 by the *Harrisburg Pennsylvanian*. But newspapers did not begin systematically reporting presidential election polls until the mid-1930s. Names such as Rensis Likert, Angus Campbell, Charles Cannell, George Gallup, and Albert Cantril were prominent in media-related research (IRS Newsletter, 1985). These individuals were among the modern innovators in quantitative research methods.

A rough delineation of the development of research techniques used in the newspaper industry would include: (1) descriptive studies reporting only percentages; (2) a variety of studies based on content analysis; (3) survey research reports using descriptive statistics; (4) survey research and content analysis using correlation statistics; (5) reports on financial and other newspaper business topics using regression statistics and analysis of variance; (6) a wide variety of studies on effects using multivariate statistics such as factor analysis, multiple-regression analysis, path analysis, and discriminant analysis. Mass communication research's reliance on data analysis by computer came as early as that by most other social science disciplines (Clevenger, 1970).

In all, the statistical and methodological advances were incorporated into newspaper research relatively quickly, as evidenced by the scholarly articles published in academic journals. There is every reason to believe those doing proprietary studies were similarly aggressive in adopting the newest research techniques.

A SYSTEMATIC APPROACH
TO WHAT WE KNOW

The scope of newspapering itself—and the associated extent of newspaper research—defies a simple scheme for following what research tells us about newspapers. Since some sort of categorization is essential, perhaps the most practical approach is organization along the same lines as the news flow process. Message gathering, or reporting procedures, is generally the point at which a story is incubated. This heading includes story ideas, the most frequent news topics, reporters and their sources, beats, and other issues associated with reporting. The next step is message encoding, or writing. This is the reporter or writer's process of putting information into story form.

The gatekeeper process comes next, including editing and managerial decisions that affect the story. Here the organizational schema becomes bloated because newsroom management itself must be included as well as what the research tells us about the business of newspapering. The message-decoding process is the next step. It involves newspaper readership—an extensive area of research, the habitual nature of newspaper uses, and the decline of newspaper use among audiences. Finally, audience effects are considered: what research tells us about how newspapers influence the reading public and society in general. As an addendum, some future considerations for newspaper research are offered.

REFERENCES

American Society of Newspaper Editors. (1985). *Newspaper credibility: Building reader trust.* Washington, DC: Author.

Baskette, F. K. & Sissors, J. Z. (1977). *The art of editing* (2nd ed.). New York: Macmillan.

Berelson, B. (1952). *Content analysis in communication research.* New York: Hafner.

Blumler, J., & Katz, E. (eds). (1974). *The uses of mass communication: Current perspectives on gratification research, Sage annual reviews of communication research* (vol. 3, pp. 20-22). Newbury Park, CA: Sage.

Bogart, L. (1968). Social sciences in the mass media. In F.T.C. Yu (Ed.), *Behavioral sciences and the mass media* (pp. 153-174). New York: Russell Sage Foundation.

[Bogart's essay goes far beyond this point in comparing the mass media and social sciences.]

Bressler, M. (1968). The potential public uses of the behavior sciences. In F.T.C. Yu (Ed.), *Behavioral sciences and the mass media*. New York: Russell Sage Foundation.

Bryant, B. E., Currier, F. P., & Morrison, A. J. (1976). Relating life style factors of person to his choice of a newspaper. *Journalism Quarterly, 53*, 74-79.

Clevenger, T., Jr. (1970). Computers and communication research. In P. Emmert & W. D. Brooks (Eds.), *Methods of research in communication*. Boston: Houghton-Mifflin.

Crespi, I. (1980). The case of presidential popularity. In A. H. Cantril (Ed.), *Polling of the issues* (pp. 28-30). Cabin John, MD: Seven Locks Press.

Crouse, T. (1973). *The boys on the bus*. New York: Random House.

Dennis, E. E., (1986, January). *Whence we came: Note on the history of communication research*. Paper presented at the Syracuse University Research Conference, Ithaca, NY.

Einsiedel, E. (1983, December 27). Comparisons of subscribers and non-subscribers. *ANPA News Research Report No. 39*.

Emery, E. (1982). Two public opinion leaders: George Gallup and Wilbur Schramm. In W. K. Agee, P. H. Ault, & E. Emery (Eds.), *Perspectives on Mass Communications* (pp. 14-17). New York: Harper & Row.

Halberstam, D. (1979). *The powers that be*. New York: Alfred A. Knopf.

Hynds, E. C. (1975). *American newspapers in the 1970s* (pp. 128-129). New York: Hastings House.

Inland Press Association. *Annual daily newspaper cost and revenue study*. Author.

IRS Newsletter. (1985, Autumn). Research profiles: Charles F. Cannell (pp. 4-5). Ann Arbor: Michigan, Institute for Social Research.

Lazarsfeld, P. F., Berelson, B., & Gaudet, H. (1944). *The people's choice*. New York: Columbia University Press.

Meyer, P. (1980). The national vs. local news controversy: A behavioral approach. *Newspaper Research Journal, 1*(2), 3-9.

Mohn, E. (1982, November 19). Morning and evening daily newspaper readers. *ANPA News Research Report No. 38*.

Rogers, J. (1918). *Newspaper building*. New York: Harper & Brothers.

Schramm, W. (1963). The challenge to communication research. In R. D. Nafziger & D. M. White (Eds.), *Introduction to mass communications research*. Baton Rouge, LA: Louisiana State University Press.

Stamm, K. R. (1985). *Newspaper use and community ties: Toward a dynamic theory*. Norwood, NJ: Ablex.

2

SECURING

NEWSPAPER CONTENT

> Securing newspaper content includes a variety of research on information gathering: reporters and their sources, the wire services, editorials, public relations' contributions, and a variety of special-interest-material providers.

One basic element of journalism is the process of gathering information for publication. There are at least two key players—the source and the reporter—and a host of supporting cast members including the major providers of messages to newspapers: the wire services, public relations practitioners, and the special content providers such as editorialists, columnists, and cartoonists. The research offers some insight on each of these information-gathering elements that result in messages disseminated by newspapers.

REPORTERS AND SOURCES

A recent ANPA literature review (Singletary, 1980) is a compendium of past research on reporters and their sources of information. This area of newspaper research usually focuses on reporter-source interaction as seen through the accuracy of news stories—the result of this process. Singletary's article, with its extensive documentation, is the source for material not specifically referenced here and can lead interested readers to the original research work.

In all, the research on reporters and sources provides a wide range of insights, although the level of accuracy in newspaper stories remains in doubt.

> Sources say about half the stories attributed to them contain errors, and most of these claimed errors are subjective rather than factual. Reporters agree that about half the source-claimed *factual* errors are really mistakes, but they rarely agree with source-claimed *subjective* errors.

Tillinghast (1983) cited research showing between 40% and 60%—about one-half—of all straight news stories are said by sources to contain at least one error. Two-thirds of the errors were considered subjective, while one-third were considered objective. Of those stories with errors, sources reported an average of 2.5 mistakes each. Tillinghast (1982) noted reporters agreed with sources' assessment of factual errors in about one-half the instances; however, reporters agreed with only 5% of the source error claims in subjective material. Generally, reporters over age 35 and those with 10 or more years journalism experience were likely to agree they had made mistakes, while younger and less-experienced reporters agreed to having made mistakes in only 15% of source error claims. The research showed no relationship between reporter age and experience and whether a story would be cited by sources for mistakes. So all classifications of reporters seem equally likely to make mistakes, but the older and more experienced reporters are more likely to concede having made one.

Tillinghast's study showed sources were more likely to claim that errors were made in stories about local government or general news and in longer stories. He found deadline pressure had an inverse effect on accuracy: The tighter the deadline, the more likely the story would be accurate. However, he attributed the effect to tighter deadlines on the afternoon daily he studied and to that particular newsroom's policy of reporter cooperation in working deadline stories. One-third of specialized beat stories (education, labor, and so forth) contained errors and 40% of police and court beat stories contained errors, compared with nearly 60% of local government and general news stories.

> Sources say beat reporters, perhaps because of their expertise or because sources know them, make fewer story errors; sources are likely to claim error in non-beat stories.

Tillinghast's study indicated sources were more likely to claim errors: (1) when they had little contact with the reporter and news media generally; (2) when multiple sources were included in a story—the two sources may have provided conflicting information; and (3) when sources were dissatisfied with the information because it seemed incomplete, connoted a less positive image, or held them up to negative public or peer reaction. Reporters were likely to agree with the source's contention of error when the information was provided by the source, referred to the source, or conflicted with the source's area of expertise. The researcher concluded source-claimed errors in news stories were largely a state of mind. Hence the 40% to 60% error rate may be overstated.

An earlier study (Griggs & Carter, 1954) looked at reporter and editor explanations for source-alleged inaccuracies. Here nearly three-fourths of the errors were objective, and only 11% were said to be a "difference of opinion between reporter and source." The newspaper's personnel chiefly attributed errors to: (1) carelessness and haste of reporters, (2) errors in written material used, (3) reporter's misunderstanding of source, (4) source-reporter semantic disagreement, and (5) a host of other explanations. This study found far more objective errors and far fewer subjective errors than the other studies, but it too showed newsroom personnel are not quick to say they made a mistake. The study suggested errors are caused by communication problems among sources and newspeople and from carelessness and lack of sufficient questioning.

Generally, the research on reporters and sources provides the following insights:

> newspaper reporters, while they may be trained observers and information providers, are subject to the same foibles that affect everyone's ability to accurately assess any situation.

Anticipated stories (press conferences and meetings) are likely to be more accurately covered than unanticipated stories (breaking news events). However, subjective errors (those of meaning and interpretation) are likely to be higher for anticipated stories, while the reporter's preparation time seems to have no effect on objective errors (mechanical and factual).

Reporters and news sources agree subjective errors are related to reporters' insufficient backgrounding and problems in the editing process. Sources have said reporters dramatize, sensationalize, overemphasize in phrasing, and rely too little on personal contact with sources. Reporters blame errors on having too little time and other reporter's laziness and incompetency.

> Sources claim a close working relationship with reporters reduces errors, and they say a press release is the best way to get error-free information into print.

While Tillinghast says prior accuracy research indicates close reporter-source contact reduces source-perceived errors, other studies show a reporter-source personal interview to be the least accurate newsgathering situation. In instances when the reporter served as an "editor," writer, or observer at an event, stories were 71% accurate. When the reporter was "involved" in the story (conference or telephone interview), stories were only 37% accurate. Stories in sports and society sections of a newspaper were found to be 77% and 90% error-free, respectively. The researcher noted most stories from these sections were nonparticipant and reporters were also more specialized, hence better able to anticipate events. Another study found student reporters made errors of omission, underemphasis, and quotes in participant-type situations.

In a study of newspeople and their sources, Carter (1958) found the reporter-source relationship is affected by: (1) images of self and others, (2) occupational stereotypes, (3) conformity to group norms and expectations, and (4) the chance selection of being a news source rather than frequent interaction with reporters. Carter said the most favorable interactions between his journalists and sources occurred when journalists "played back" their work to check for completeness and accuracy and when the two reached a commonality on technical language.

> Reporters are prone to biases that manifest themselves in articles on social issues, on topics on which the reporter has strong personal views, and on stories about deviant groups.

Other studies indicate subjective errors are more likely to occur in social issue reporting as opposed to straight news reports. Of 193 social issue stories, only 31% were error-free, an accuracy rate approximating that of science news reporting. The finding showed complicated topics are more difficult to cover than general news. Likewise, a reporter's bias will interfere with accuracy: Reporters with strong views on a topic will make more subjective errors. When reporter views are in conflict with the event being covered, reporting is slower, less accurate, and less readable. When reporters are in conflict with sources and feel themselves objects of manipulation, writing styles change to reduce conflict: reporters seek ways to write the story "safely."

Related to the bias question was a study by Shoemaker (1983) that concluded journalists' stories about deviant sociopolitical groups actually contain negative *unattributed* nouns and adjectives. She found—contrary to the journalistic convention of maintaining objectivity, especially in unattributed references—the more deviant the group, the more unfavorable unattributed references were. Attributed references to deviant groups' spokespersons were found to be neutral, and both types of references to deviant groups indicated the reporters portrayed such groups as less legitimate than nondeviant groups.

> Crises stories are likely to contain errors.

Disaster or crisis story reporting was found to be error-prone, to the extent that editors may wish to concede the possibility such articles may contain errors and to make such a concession in the story itself. Crisis stories imply more reporter stress. Research has shown reporters are subject to error in stressful reporting and writing situations. With reporter stress, stories: (1) take longer to write, (2) are less complete, (3) have more errors, and (4) are less readable.

A few recent studies have investigated the broader implications of newspaper reporting during crises. Shapiro and Williams (1984) compared coverage by the local press and that by more distant newspapers during a civil disturbance in Miami. They found newspapers closest to the scene of a violent incident provided more information but were likely to downplay the violent aspects of the accident. The researchers said editors' concern for the local market results in selecting information that helps readers understand the local implications of crisis events. Ledingham and Masel-Walters (1985) looked at the Galveston media's reporting of a hurricane and citizens' response to media warnings. The researchers urged local media to enter into a cooperative, preevent crisis plan with local officials to improve information flow of public warnings in future crisis situations. Wilkins (1985) investigated media coverage of a blizzard that struck Denver in 1982. He found the media content focused on a theme of helplessness against nature and devoted more space to coverage to the blizzard itself—the event—rather than to warnings or community preparedness. In all, the research on crisis reporting suggests that broad newspaper coverage of a crisis is as open to misinformation as individual reporters' crisis stories are to factual error.

A reporter's personality traits and mind set can influence story accuracy.

A reporter's own neurosis—competition, fear of failure, distrust of others—can lead to information distortion, particularly understatement and overstatement. While some researchers speculated reporter error would generally tend to be exaggeration rather than minimization, the findings showed error to be evenly balanced in both directions. While being neurotic rather than stable resulted in errors, there was no difference in error rates between introverted and extroverted personality types.

Closed- and open-minded reporter types have been studied with the expectation that closed-minded (more authoritarian or dogmatic) people will produce stories more likely to be perceived as inaccurate. More closed-minded people were also found to take longer to complete a task inconsistent with their ideals.

A study of newswriters' fantasies of their audiences indicated two types of writer: those whose image was "joy" in writing for an approving audience and those whose image was "combat" in writing for an antag-onistic audience. When the news, either good or bad, was incongruent with the writer's audience fantasy, accuracy suffered. Bad news tended to be more distorted than good. Other studies found reporters color stories to conform to their expectations of the audience's likely pre-disposition toward the message. If a reporter thought readers would be opposed to the message, reporter stress during the writing process might impede an accurate portrayal.

Other than the extensive research on accuracy of news stories, few studies on reporters and their sources exist. Those that do take a variety of approaches.

One study (Dansker, Wilcox, & Van Tubergen, 1980) tried to deter-mine how reporters evaluate the credibility of their sources. Using a sample of Investigative Reporters and Editors (IRE), the researchers identified three types of reporters: those who reject intuition as a basis of judging source credibility, those who are neutral about intuition, and those who do use intuition as a guide. The IRE members provided these guidelines by which to judge a source's credibility, in this order of importance: (1) past record of the source's reliability, (2) the source's rea-sons for providing information, (3) "gut feeling," (4) source's ability to produce documentation, and (5) ability to corroborate source's material.

Ryan (1982) matched the opinions of newspaper science writers with sources for science news, a set of scientists who had little recent contact with reporters and a set of scientists who had frequent contact with reporters. He found: (1) scientists with high contact were no different from those with low contact in their ability to predict reporters' views on handling science news; (2) higher- and lower-contact sources were equally distant from journalists' views about science news writing; and (3) high- and low-contact sources had virtually the same views about science news coverage. Ryan concluded increased press contact does not improve a source's understanding of the news-gathering and writing processes. He suggested that reporters need to do a better job of explain-ing their work to sources before trying to educate the general public.

What should be evident from this review of findings about sources and reporters is that the research has concentrated on story accuracy. It ignores most other aspects of the reporter-source information-gathering process. True, journalism textbooks on reporting offer hundreds of suggestions and thousands of words on how to report, but it is clear that little of what is being taught can be based on comprehensive studies of the reporting process.

Consider a study about newspaper science writers reporting from a national convention of the American Association for the Advancement of Science (AAAS; Dunwoody, 1979). The author identified a formal organization of science writers, the National Association of Science Writers, Inc., and an "inner club" of journalists who wrote for the elite mass media. She found that organizational constraints—deadlines, competition, and technical equipment needs—adversely influenced reporters' news gathering by forcing them to rely more on press conferences and fewer sources per story. Those without such constraints, who usually worked for print media, attended and reported more of the AAAS meeting sessions rather than relying on press conferences. Inner-club members shared information and helped one another gather and interpret the news. Inner-club members' stories were more accurate and of higher quality. The same kinds of findings were made by Grey (1966) in his case study of a Supreme Court reporter. Shields and Dunwoody found similar effects in a study of Wisconsin reporters (1986), as did Atwater and Fico in their 1986 study of Michigan state-house reporters.

These recent studies certainly go beyond the single aspect of accuracy in news reporting. They deal with the reporting process and they identify a host of variables unlikely to be included in reporting textbooks. These research projects should significantly increase both reporters' and editors' understanding of the dimensions of news gathering. While it is unfortunate such examples of practical research on the reporting process have been undertaken only recently, there is every indication this trend will continue.

WIRE SERVICE INFORMATION

A daily newspaper's news columns rely heavily on the output of the Associated Press (AP) and United Press International (UPI), as well as on that of several news services offered through newspaper groups. Just how much of daily newspapers' content is provided by wire services is a matter of some speculation since the percentage seems to vary.

Of AP and UPI, research has shown most editors agree AP is more reliable but UPI's writing is brighter (Liebs, 1966); AP is conservative and UPI is somewhat faster in news handling, and there has been a trend against use of multiple wire services by newspapers (Schwarzlose, 1966). Also, and rather obvious in the mid-1980s, UPI is in financial straits and struggling to reposition itself as a more effective information provider (Stepp, 1984). Trayes (1972) found the AP was used by two out of three dailies, UPI was used by nearly one-half, and the remaining wire use by frequency was the *New York Times Service*, the *Chicago Daily News Service*, Reuters, and Dow Jones. He noted that newspaper size was not a reliable predictor of the number of news or feature services a particular daily might take. A more recent study of supplemental news services (Littlewood & DeLong, 1981) showed the dominant ones, by number of subscribers, were New York *Times,* Los Angeles *Times,* Washington *Post, Field News Service,* and *Knight News Tribune.*

An early study (Barnes, 1951) showed that in coverage of a sensational murder trial, radio wires were tamer than press wires and the study's respondents rated press wire service coverage of the trial to be more in poor taste than offensive, although wire story statements got the same ranking on scales of offensiveness and poor taste.

> Wire stories, particularly the top news stories, are used by daily newspapers and get favorable play. In fact, newspaper wire editors' production schedules work against their making selection decisions, hence the wires actually determine much of what will be published simply by their decisions of what they transmit to newspapers.

The seminal study of wire editors as gatekeepers was that by White (1950) who concluded that a wire editor's selection of content was determined by his space limitations, his concept of newsworthiness, and his personal biases. Snider (1967) replicated the study with the same wire editor. The researcher reported the newspaper took fewer wire services in the mid-1960s, but the same editor's pattern of news selection remained unchanged. Still, major research findings over time have been that a wire editor's technological constraints of production and time—rather than news value judgments of any type—result in the wires actually determining what will appear by the content they feed.

Gieber (1956), in a study of 16 wire editors, described his subjects as being too busy with mechanical details of production to be active screeners of wire copy. He found AP playing an important role in selecting the news by determining what was sent to its member papers. Although deskpeople said they emphasized stories they thought were important to the greatest number of their readers, Gieber said that these wire editors' news values were nebulous and that they did not screen wire copy critically. Likewise Shaw (1969) found technological factors such as newshole space prevented newspaper wire editors from making critical selection judgments. The relationship between incoming wire news and wire news carried in papers was so strong that AP and UPI wire editors can be viewed as determining what will be news for a community on any given day.

On the other hand, an investigation of AP and UPI copy provided to newspapers on the Cuban revolt (Lewis, 1960) showed the wires had provided sufficient coverage, but the wire editors of four dailies had not used much of the copy. Failure to use copy was due to lack of available space and the belief that their readers had provincial views precluding audience interest in news from Latin America until the revolt reached crisis stages. Hence in this instance, at the four papers studied, wire editors had made a decision not to use specific categories of wire content. Cutlip (1954) found that AP writers on four Wisconsin dailies filed 100,000 words per day, 57,000 of which were selected by AP editors. About 13,350 words were selected by state AP trunk editors, and 6,000 more words on state news were added for subscriber paper feeds. Of 122 items received at the papers, the dailies used an average of 74 items. One-fifth of the total items were from Washington, DC, and 40% of the content dealt with governmental stories.

In a study of AP wire copy use by 19 Minnesota dailies, Casey (1958) found 59% of the wire copy sent in one day was used, and larger papers used more wire copy than did smaller papers. Rejection claims included: lack of space, lack of reader interest, lack of news value or significance, late arrival, equipment or equipment operator problems, and editorial problems such as makeup. A similar study (Clark, 1960) of AP copy use in 24 Iowa evening papers during a 10-day period found that with four exceptions, less than one-half the wire copy was used. The researcher said lack of use depended on subject matter categories, but there was no consistent pattern of nonuse by subject. At least one-half the wire budget stories used appeared on page one or the paper's jump page. Rejecting wire stories was achieved by eliminating the entire story. Gold (1965), in a similar study of Iowa dailies, found use of wire copy ranged from about 5% to almost 57% of available copy; however, the papers varied little from each other and from the AP feed in the relative emphasis they gave to wire copy received. And Jones (1961) found that timeliness was a significant factor in use of wire service copy by 23 Minnesota afternoon papers. Roughly 36% of the available copy was used, and 92% went into print on the same day the stories were filed. Only about 10% of out-of-state datelined copy was used, but 19% of Washington, DC, copy with a Minnesota slant was used. The researcher speculated that editors were not actually reading all copy but were making decisions based on wire story datelines. Stempel's study (1964) of how afternoon dailies use the wire indicated that nearly 70% of all wire copy appearing in the 20 large papers he analyzed was run in the first editions, and nearly one-half of these stories appeared in subsequent editions just as they were published in the first. Conversely, only 15% of the wire items sent after 10 a.m. were used because of the growing availability of locally produced copy.

Stempel (1959) studied standardization in six Michigan dailies served by UPI. He found that only 8 of 764 stories used by the dailies were used by all six papers in the same way, but that 31% of the stories were used similarly by the papers. He concluded that the wires do not necessarily standardize newspaper presentation of news, but combined with other conditions the wires do contribute to the standardization process.

Whitney and Becker (1982) performed a field experiment with 46 editors in Ohio. Editors were offered a balanced menu of wire stories (14.3% in each of seven news subject categories) and another menu of stories in proportion to what wires have been reported to actually provide. The researchers concluded editors' selection process is relatively "uncritical"; they accept news in the same proportions it is provided by the wires. While much of the research indicates the wires have tremendous influence in setting editors' agenda for the categories of news stories carried, there is also evidence to the contrary. Stempel (1985) looked at the general question of news selection—all longer national and international news stories in nine national media over a four-day period. He found similarity among media in the broad categories of news selected but little agreement in specific stories actually used. Newspaper news was different from television news, and there were different patterns of news found among the six papers in the study. He concluded there is "a general notion as to what makes a suitable news package . . . similar to the general notion that nutrition experts have as to what makes up a suitable diet. . . . However, on just which specific items should be included there is not much agreement among either nutrition experts or news gatekeepers."

Since much of the Washington governmental coverage reported in newspapers is provided by wire services, this topic has been given special attention by researchers. Witcover (1969) found AP and UPI staffers covering Congress were overworked and made routine information collection trips to news source sites rather than providing intense reporting on government activities, as subscribers might expect. Wilhoit and Sherrill (1968) looked at AP coverage of senators and found coverage was related to senators' being from larger states and having more seniority.

In a study comparing accuracy of the two major wires, Cote (1970) found no difference in source-alleged errors between the two wires.

EDITORIALS' INFLUENCE

Studies of newspaper editorials have focused on the continuing assessment of how effective editorials are in the election process: How well do newspaper editorials influence voters? The lay reader will enjoy an article on the topic by Shaw (1977) whose overview of the issue follows research findings:

Newspaper endorsements are effective. The research generally indicates
newspaper editorials are most influential: (1) in swaying voters on local
candidates and referenda; (2) if newspapers in the same market don't
make conflicting endorsements; and (3) if a paper's endorsement is contrary to the public's expectation of what the paper's choice would have
been. Endorsements of propositions are more influential than endorsements on candidates.

Five different studies found newspaper endorsements of local candidates could deliver from 9,000 to more than 24,000 votes for the endorsed
candidate, depending on city size (Mueller, 1970). McCombs's (1967)
and Robinson's (1974) research showed editorials were at least as effective in state and national elections, accounting for about 6% of the vote.
McCombs's study indicated newspaper endorsements are most likely to
influence voters on low-profile issues and high-profile, contradictory
issues. Also, he found the last-minute deciders are likely to be influenced
by endorsements. Robinson found that in presidential elections, losing
candidates were helped more by endorsements. Hurd and Singletary's
(1984) study of the 1980 election contradicted others in determining
presidential endorsements swayed only about 1% of the electorate.
Fedler, Counts, and Stephens (1982) studied a national sample of large-
city dailies in the 1980 presidential election and found the combination
of endorsements by newspapers available in a city determined how
endorsements affect voters.

Rystrom (1986) reported the "apparent" results of endorsements by
51 California dailies on election returns from 1970 to 1980. Although the
net impact over time averaged only 1% of the votes, he noted extensive
variance for endorsements' influence, depending on the election situation. He concluded endorsements are most effective in independent
rather than group-owned papers, in smaller rather than larger papers, in
papers that are more politically moderate than extreme. Rystrom's data
indicated endorsements for propositions are more effective than for
candidate races, and they are more effective in primaries than in general
elections. He said editorials opposing issues that would cost taxpayers
money are more effective and liberal endorsements are more effective
than conservative endorsements on ideological, emotional issues. He
urged newspapers to treat primaries as thoroughly as general elections,
to concentrate on propositions, and to pay more attention to local and
regional rather than statewide issues and candidates.

If asked should papers endorse political candidates, only about one-
half the citizens polled give their support to newspaper policies that
favor making editorial endorsements (Bush, 1966: 1967).

Exit polling indicates newspaper endorsements may be even more influential than previously thought.

Until recently, the chief method of investigating endorsements' influence was to link election returns with whether endorsements had appeared in local newspapers. Another method was to survey voters before or after the election. But with exit polling, it is possible to catch voters while the ingredients that influenced their opinions are still fresh in their minds.

In one recent study (Fedler, Smith, & Counts, 1985), exit polling showed voters acknowledged newspaper editorials had been more influential in their voting choices than previous investigations had demonstrated. The Florida exit poll study found 23% of interviewees said endorsements helped them decide who to vote for, and they reported endorsements were more helpful for local elections and for propositions. Exit polls combined with a national survey (Gafke, 1982) found voters more influenced by endorsements in papers with which they usually agreed and papers they considered more prestigious. Additionally, the Gafke study found more influence by newspaper editorials when: (1) they dealt with propositions rather than candidates, (2) they were for local rather than state elections, and (3) there were no conflicting endorsements made by other papers in the market.

The Gafke study found more voter awareness of the endorsements in larger-circulation papers, more awareness by higher-education voters, and more awareness when newspapers wrote unequivocal endorsements. Finally, the Gafke study found editorial endorsements opposing a position or candidate for which the voter had already decided to vote, reinforce that voter's prior decision.

As some of the earlier researchers suggested (Coombs, 1981), the assessment of endorsements on voters' decisions seems to be a more complicated matter than merely testing for links between endorsements and vote tallies. Counts (1985) looked at these two measures while controlling for party registration, percentage of home owners, population per square mile, and population change. His research determined the relationship between endorsements and votes disappeared when the intervening variables were considered. He disagreed with most previous researchers by declaring there was no causal influence by endorsements for presidential elections. In the same year, St.Dizier (1985) described an experiment that resulted in an overwhelming shift in opinion in the direction of a newspaper endorsement. Although the test was not a valid election situation, if voters' behavior is even remotely similar to St.Dizier's findings, newspaper endorsements would be extremely influential in low-information races. While the exact influence of endorsements remains a hotly contested research issue, the weight of evidence is endorsements have at least some influence and may, under the right circumstances, swing an election.

Another area of study on editorials has received less attention. We don't really know much about the content of editorials except that it's generally conceded that the majority of daily newspapers use canned editorials (those provided by syndicated feature services) and run editorials with little vigor or bite on critical issues.

> While newspapers have been criticized for lack of vigor in local editorials, the research indicates papers under 100,000 circulation offer a higher percentage of persuasive editorials on local and state issues.

In reviewing past studies on local editorial vigor, Stempel (1979) reported four previous studies showed only one-quarter to one-half of newspaper editorials were on local issues, and that only about one-half of these took argumentative stands. Stempel's study found about 20% of all editorials were intended to persuade and for papers with circulations of under 100,000, 38% of the local and 29% of the state issue editorials were intended to persuade. While larger papers ran more editorials, smaller papers had more editorials that took a stand on local issues.

SPECIAL COLUMNS

Beyond news and editorials, most dailies provide a considerable diet of columns of special reader interest, much of which is nationally syndicated. A few researchers have looked at this special content with the observations described below.

Anderson (1982) looked at the content of Jack Anderson's "Washington Merry-Go-Round" and found this political column (taken by more than 1,000 newspapers) presented diverse coverage of current events in 1980. Topics receiving more than 10% of the total inches published were President Carter, Congress, general international, and general federal government. But there were 10 other categories of issues receiving at least 2% of total inches published and 8 more categories included that received less than 100 column inches. The researcher said readers were "provided with a broad overview of political affairs," and he rejected criticism that the column was repetitious and focused on obscure news subjects.

In an overview of political columnists, Hynds (1980) noted virtually all dailies use them on the editorial or op-ed page. His survey showed 93% of papers used editorial columns for political analysis, 75% for political reporting, 63% for humor, 33% for business, 20% for religion, 13% for advice, and 1% for gossip. Bagdikian (1964; see also 1966) said there was a mounting trend by papers to use political columnists for balancing editorial views, and Hynds found 61% of surveyed editors agreeing that they selected these columnists to balance conservative and liberal views. Leading columnists on the left were Jack Anderson, James Reston, Tom Wicker, Joseph Kraft, and Nicholas Von Hoffman; on the right were James J. Kilpatrick, William F. Buckley, and George Will. David Broder and Jack Anderson were mentioned for their reporting, and Art Buchwald dominated the humorist category.

Locally produced columns of book reviews have received some attention from researchers. A survey of newspaper book review editors in 1959 was compared with one in 1980 (Himebaugh & Kennedy), and researchers found that with the passage of time more book review sections were relegated to Sunday-only; fewer papers ran a full page of reviews; more papers imposed length limitations; and fewer papers were running best-seller lists. While locally produced reviews dropped, papers using syndicated reviews climbed from 20% to 55%, and papers running local literary news coverage outside the book review section increased from 40% to 71%. Further, more editors in 1980 said they targeted book reviews to special reader audiences, made an effort to balance between fiction and nonfiction, and were more likely to publish evaluative reviews. While in the early study writing ability was the chief criterion for selecting reviewers, in 1980 it was background knowledge. Methods of handling book reviews that did not change during the 20-year period were having categories of books editors refused to review (vanity press, highly specialized topics, and pornographic books); the actual length of reviews (400-500 words) and total column inches devoted to them (6-10 columns); fairness; and the criteria for review content (plot summary, evaluation of style, judgment of worth to the average reader, and information about the author).

Wyatt and Haskins's (1985) national sample of book review editors by circulation size determined the volume of reviews published increased with circulation, as did the number of regular reviewers. He found average weekly space devoted to reviews to be between three-fourths of a page and a full page, and locally produced reviews to be 71% of the total. Only one-fifth of the editors handle reviews full-time. Editors are most commonly male (62%), between age 30 and 40 (53%), and hold master's degrees (59%). Nearly one-fourth are authors of books. They are generally not active in national book associations.

Wyatt found categories of books getting priority were biography, history, serious fiction, and politics and government. The larger the newspaper, the more review books it is likely to receive. But editors rate only one-third appropriate for review and another one-fourth marginally appropriate. The following criteria, in the order given, were the top reasons for selecting a book to review: subject, editor's interest, author, local appearance of author, national award, best seller, and receiving a review copy.

TEENS' CONTENT

Special teens' content is another newspaper content area that has received some investigation, although not very recently. Lyle (1968) surveyed ANPA-member newspapers and reported 57% published either columns, pages, or sections aimed at youth. Almost all were published weekly and were aimed at senior high school and college or junior and senior high school students. Youth pages and sections contained pictures and some ads, but not many. Editors said among the chief purposes in running youth material were: (1) to develop the newspaper reading habit among youngsters, 66%; (2) because youth is a part of the audience and deserves coverage, 30%; and (3) youth needs a forum of its own, 14%. Student-written or syndicated matter accounted for 43% of the section content, 48% of the youth-pages content, and 53% of the column content.

Lyle did a content analysis of the values in youth-department content and determined 30% dealt with sports activity, 29% with achievement or recognition, 20% with new experiences or creative self-expression, and 16% with knowledge. In all, only about 5% of values presented were considered moral.

> It's unclear whether youth news should be concentrated in a youth section
> or spread throughout the newspaper with general news items. While teens
> give high readership to youth sections, they also give more attention than
> adults to their special interest items throughout the paper.

In Lyle's study, not all the editors were happy with their youth content. Some wanted to reduce school news and increase coverage of topics and opinions on youth interests, but editors said they were unable to detect a trend in the kind of content that might interest youth. This seemed evident from the actual content being run: While 20-25% of the content was general school news, about 56% was entertainment or miscellaneous. Other editors (of 24 papers) said they were considering abandoning the separate youth sections in favor of mixing youth news with general news in the paper, and one said the paper's readership studies supported the mix strategy.

However, a survey of 17 newspapers (Carl J. Nelson Research, 1968) provided readership percentages for youth sections in two of the papers, reporting teens were more likely than adults to read the content of these sections. And the Richmond papers (1967), in a random survey, reported the only newspaper content areas teens read more than adults were some sports coverage, high school roundup, college roundup, "Motorsport Report," radio and TV listings, movie and theater reviews, the "Ask Andy" column, "Junior Editors," and the weekly youth page. The *Tribune* (South Bend, Indiana, 1971) polled teens about its Sunday high school pages and found "every Sunday" readership jumped nearly 12% for boys and nearly 19% for girls between 1963 and 1969. Campbell (1971) queried high school students in five states and found the highest readership for comics, their high school sports, movie ads, personal advice columns, other news of their high school, and news about teens and juveniles. And in a large sample of Texas high school students, Davis and Watkins (1967) found males and females combined would be at least very interested in advice for following a career, current news that affects teenagers, and advice for going to college. While these Texas students reported their local paper was scattering youth news (55%) instead of giving it assigned space (37%), their preference was for a daily column (62%), a weekly page (28%), or scattered (10%).

There is actually little reason to debate the ability of youth sections to catch teens' interest, and today's newspaper manager must disregard as well a survey (ANPA, 1969) showing teenage columns and sections were among the largest item-use gainers in newspapers studied between 1952 and 1967. According to the most recent figures cited by Bogard (1981), newspapers cut back on using specialized features between 1967 and 1979, and teenage features were deleted more than any other type. Some 61% of papers carried teen pages in 1967, 45% ran them in 1974, and only 24% of papers still had them in 1979.

CARTOONS AND COMICS

Another area of newspaper research interest—particularly because high readership has been so well documented—is the cartoon or comic sections.

Studies by Brinkman (1968) and Carl (1968) indicate editorial cartoons are not as influential as editorials, and only 15% of readers fully understood editorial cartoons' messages. A recent inquiry about political cartoonists (Hynds, 1979) indicates political cartooning is regaining its stature as polemical criticism (Dennis, 1974), and the current syndicated leaders are Herblock, Oliphant, and MacNelly. Hynds' survey found almost all cartoonists today are men (98%), in their 40s and 50s (63%). Self-professed middle-of-the-roaders account for 36%; liberals, 32%; and conservatives, 19%. However, 63% are political independents, 19% are Republicans, and 12% are Democrats. No conservatives say they work for liberal papers, but 29% of the liberals say their papers are conservative. Although nearly one-half declined to pick a chief function that they see for their work, the remainder gave the following responses from among several choices:

Make people think	95%
Entertain	75%
Express concern	73%
Illustrate problems	67%
Call for change	63%

Two-thirds said cartoons should express the author's opinion, not the newspaper's, although 21% opted for the institutional opinion. Nearly three-fourths said cartoonists should develop their own ideas rather than complement editorials. Most of the cartoonists said there aren't many really good practitioners in the field today, perhaps fewer than 25 top persons. They cited absence of controversy and worn-out ideas, poor drawing, and failure to understand the subject as problems. They noted trends in cartooning as less use of stereotypes, complicated drawings, and complicated captions and more use of color.

Riffe, Sneed, and Rogers (1985a) replicated Hynds's study of cartoonists and found cartoonists were younger, less likely to be politically independent and more likely to be Democrats, and less productive when measured by the number of cartoons drawn. The chief roles cartoonists attributed to themselves were critic, artist, and opinion leader. Riffe compared cartoonists' views with their editors' views and found general agreement on what the cartoonist's role is and should be, although cartoonists opted for more autonomy than editors thought they should have. There was general agreement between cartoonists and editors on what constitutes a good editorial cartoon.

In a follow-up study, Riffe, Sneed, and Rogers (1985b) reported editorial cartoonists believed their political views were different from those of the newspaper they represented—cartoonists thought their views were more liberal than their newspaper's. Editors knew their cartoonists felt this way, but the research showed cartoonists were significantly more liberal on economic and defense issues only.

Comics, although they don't usually qualify as serious commentary, have nonetheless received considerable attention from newspaper researchers because of their reader following. We know the audience for comics is both large and intense.

> People are first drawn to newspaper reading through the comics section, and while their interest wanes with age, the comics continue to receive quite high average readership compared with any other newspaper content.

Since Schramm and White (1949) did their landmark study of newspaper-item readership and age level, research has always documented that youngsters and teenagers begin the newspaper-reading habit through the comics. Interests in sports and news broadens with age. A typical readership finding (Milwaukee *Journal*, 1966) is that more than 95% of readers under 18 read the Sunday comics, and the percentage drops steadily for age cohorts until it reaches about 40% at age 65 and older. While people say they think comic readers are in the lower socioeconomic strata, comic readers are relatively equally represented in all occupational categories except farmers and retired-widowed (Robinson & White, 1967). Further, every-week reading of comics increases with education up to college graduate, at which point it declines slightly. These findings for the Sunday comics are true as well for weekday comic section readership.

RELIGION AND CHURCH PAGES

Among the general adult reading population, interest in the church page or religion news is not a priority, but this content does get considerably high ratings compared with other specialized content. Readers are likely to say it's important regardless of their actual readership (Bogart, 1981).

Root and Bolder (1966) found 37% of church-oriented readers usually read the church page and the most church-oriented preferred organized church news and information, while others preferred personalities and feature stories. Rarick (1967) studied readers of the Salem (Oregon) *Capital Journal* and determined 37% were frequent church-page readers. He found more frequent churchgoers were more frequent readers, and men were similar to women in their church attendance and church-page readership.

A recent study of Huntington, West Virginia, newspaper readers (Buddenbaum, 1982) found 42% said they were frequent readers of news and religion. These frequent religion readers were female, active in a church, older, less educated, in lower socioeconomic groups, and were more likely to be housewives, retired, and unemployed persons. Buddenbaum's figures show single people are not likely to read religion news; 36% of married, 44% of divorced or separated, and 93% of widowed persons do. She found religion readers have a conservative value orientation. God-oriented religion readers' associated newspaper reading is local and of immediate personal concern, and they are similar to the audience for religious television programs. Information-oriented religion readers also read more general news and opinion content. Buddenbaum recommended keeping the religion page separate for those who consider it vital and including more religious dimensions in appropriate straight news stories throughout the paper while developing related local people features for the religion page. Swain (1982), studying the coverage by 16 metropolitan papers of a religion story on married Catholic priests, found the most accurate coverage was by those papers that had a religion specialist who handled the story.

PUBLIC RELATIONS' CONTRIBUTION

As our society has become more conscious of communication generally, researchers have turned more to analysis of the role of public relations as an information provider for newspapers. While it long has been recognized that much of the flow of communication to the news media has been through public relations releases, a recent trend away from news releases and toward media relations has drawn the attention of newspaper researchers. Every newspaper editor is aware of the stream of releases that crosses the news desk daily; but, while this deluge continues, a more subtle source relationship now exists between public relations and the news media. It occurs through personal contact and telephone calls to the growing number of corporate and agency public relations practitioners who act as intermediaries between news gatherers and official sources, and who therefore do serve as news flow gatekeepers.

Regular news sources believe distributing news releases is the way to ensure published information will be accurate.

It has already been noted that sources believe accuracy of published news reports is highest when stories are based on press releases rather than on reporter-source interviews. Apparently sources believe media stories are likely to contain fewer objective errors and to be more comprehensive if news writers use a written release as the primary basis of an article.

> Journalists say the use of public relations material is a decision based on its news value, but research indicates public relations practitioners' influence goes beyond the news value criterion.

Many of the studies on journalists' use of public relations releases have identified news value as the chief decision point in whether a given item's content will reach publication (see Aronoff, 1976). Much of the public relations research has shown that practitioners' activities do influence news flow. Whether the publicist actually dictates media content, or whether journalists' news value decisions dominate, is still a matter of debate. Sachsman (1976) studied 200 environmental news articles and determined 53% were from public relations sources, and one-half of these were rewritten press releases. And while Dunwoody and Ryan (1983) found scientists denied that public information officers influenced most stories written about them, the researchers speculated these scientists didn't necessarily understand how influential public information officers were.

Stocking (1985) found traditional news values, rather than public information activity, accounted for more national media content on medical research. She found some evidence, however, that public information officers were having a more subtle effect on news content through their "reactive" role of responding to the initial contacts made by national media. She speculated additionally that local media would place more reliance on public relations activities than national media.

A recent study by VanSlyke Turk (1986) examined the activity of six state agency public information offices in Louisiana. She found that half the information subsidies released by these agencies did appear in newspapers. However, the releases accounted for only half the information that appeared on the six agencies. So newspaper reporters were contacting sources directly in half the cases. While VanSlyke Turk found acceptance of released information was related to the media's perception of each agency's newsworthiness—the journalists did exercise news value control—the copy based on releases that appeared in print, mirrored the substance of output from agency releases. The conclusion here is that when journalists rely primarily on news releases, agencies will succeed in getting their intended message in print. Finally, this study suggested a straight news treatment in releases will be more acceptable to newspapers than releases that contain the organization's point of view or "spin."

CONCLUSIONS

While the research offers scant information about the accuracy of reporters and sources, there is some evidence about accuracy in news stories resulting from the reporter-source relationship. There is also evidence of a recent trend toward research that may improve understanding about how reporters function in the information-gathering process. But there has been considerable research on several other aspects of information gathering for newspapers: the information that makes its way into print but does not include reporter-source news gathering. Included are studies about the wire services and their impact on newspapers' content, editorial endorsements and their influence, the work of syndicated columnists and cartoonists, teen- and religion-page content in newspapers, and the role of public relations practitioners in providing media information.

Although the content provided here is certainly not a complete list of the information newspapers gather and publish—no mention is made of letters to the editor, the business pages, sports, movie reviews, advice columns, and other similar content categories—it does offer an overview of much of the news-gathering process. The research neglects appraising how much of a daily newspaper's content can be attributed to each of these providers. We may assume the percentage of content has changed over time, as in the case of teens' pages, but it is evident that a newspaper relies on a host of non-staff-produced material to fill its columns and interest its audience. Perhaps the most significant finding from this review of information gathering is the gap in knowledge about how reporters work with sources. It is, after all, the most critical element in providing information to the news-reading public, and it is probably the single aspects of newsroom operations editors could manage that would result in improved quality of the product.

REFERENCES

Reporters and Sources

Atwater, T., & Fico, F. (1986). Source reliance and use in reporting state government: A study of print and broadcast practices. *Newspaper Research Journal, 8*(1), 53.

Carter, R. E., Jr. (1958). Newspaper "gatekeepers" and the sources of news. *Public Opinion Quarterly, 22*, 133-144.

Dansker, E., Wilcox, J. R., & Van Tubergen, G. N. (1980). How reporters evaluate the credibility of their sources. *Newspaper Research Journal, 1*(2), 40.

Dunwoody, S. (1979). News-gathering behaviors of specialty reporters: A two-level comparison of mass media decision-making. *Newspaper Research Journal, 1*(1), 29.

Grey, D. L. (1966). Decision-making by a reporter under deadline pressure. *Journalism Quarterly, 43*, 419-428.

Griggs, H. H., & Carter, N. (1964, June). Why reporting errors? *The Florida Press.*

Ledingham, J. A., & Masel-Walters, L. (1985). Written on the Wind: The Media and Hurricane Alicia. *Newspaper Research Journal, 6*(2), 50.

Ryan, M. (1982). Impact of personal contact on sources' views of the press. *Newspaper Research Journal, 3*(3), 22.

Shapiro, M., & Williams, J., Jr. (1984). Civil disturbance in Miami: Proximity and conflict in newspaper coverage. *Newspaper Research Journal, 5*(3), 61.

Shields, S., & Dunwoody, S. (1986). The social world of the statehouse pressroom. *Newspaper Research Journal, 8*(1), 43.

Shoemaker, P. J. (1983). Bias and source attribution. *Newspaper Research Journal, 5*(1), 25.

Singletary, M. (1980, January 25). Accuracy in news reporting: A review of the research. *ANPA News Research Report No. 25.*

Stempel, G. H., III. (1985). Gatekeeping: The mix of topics and the selection of stories. *Journalism Quarterly, 62*, 791-796, 815.

Tillinghast, W. A. (1982, July 29). Newspaper errors: Source perception, reporter response and some causes. *ANPA News Research Report No. 35.*

Tillinghast, W. A. (1983). Source control and evaluation of newspaper inaccuracies. *Newspaper Research Journal, 5*(1), 13.

Wilkins, L. (1985). Television and newspaper coverage of a blizzard: Is the message helplessness? *Newspaper Research Journal, 6*(4), 51.

Wire Service Information

Barnes, A. M. (1951). How wire services reported the Rutledge murder trial: A study in taste. *Journalism Quarterly, 28*, 161-178.

Carter, R. E., Jr. (1958). Newspaper "Gatekeepers" and the sources of news. *Public Opinion Quarterly, 22*, 133-144.

Casey, R. D. (1958). Use of foreign news by 19 Minnesota dailies. *Journalism Quarterly, 35*, 87-89.

Clark, J. A. (1960). *A study of the use of wire service copy by Iowa evening newspapers which receive wire service copy only from the Iowa-Nebraska circuit of the Associated Press.* Unpublished dissertation, University of Iowa.

Cote, J. R. (1970). A study of accuracy of two wire services. *Journalism Quarterly, 47*, 660-666.

Cutlip, S. M. (1954). Content and flow of AP news—from trunk to TTS to reader. *Journalism Quarterly, 31*, 434-446.

Gieber, W. (1956). Across the desk: A study of 16 telegraph editors. *Journalism Quarterly, 33*, 423-442.

Gold, D. (1965). News selection patterns among Iowa dailies. *Public Opinion Quarterly, 29*, 425-430.

Jones, R. L., Trohldahl, V. C., & Hvistendahl, J. K. (1961). News selection patterns from a state-TTS wire. *Journalism Quarterly, 38,* 303-312.

Lewis, H. L. (1960). The Cuban revolt story: AP, UPI and 3 papers. *Journalism Quarterly, 37,* 573-578.

Liebes, B. H. (1966). Decision-making by telegraph editors—AP or UPI? *Journalism Quarterly, 43,* 434-442.

Littlewood, T. B., & DeLong, R. (1981). Supplemental news services. *Newspaper Research Journal, 2*(4), 9.

Schwarzlose, R. A. (1966). Trends in U.S. newspapers' wire service resources, 1934-66. *Journalism Quarterly, 43,* 627-638.

Shaw, D. L. (1969). Surveillance vs. constraint: Press coverage of a social issue. *Journalism Quarterly, 46,* 707-712.

Snider, P. B. (1967). "Mr. Gates" revisited: A 1966 version of the 1949 case study. *Journalism Quarterly, 44,* 419-427.

Stempel, G. H., III. (1959). Uniformity of wire content of six Michigan dailies. *Journalism Quarterly, 36,* 45-48, 129.

Stempel, G. H., III. (1964). How newspapers use the Associated Press afternoon A-wire. *Journalism Quarterly, 41,* 380-384.

Stempel, G. H., III. (1985). Gatekeeping: The mix of topics and the selection of stories. *Journalism Quarterly, 62,* 791-796, 815.

Stepp, C. S. (1984). Redefining the news service: An analysis of change at United Press International. *Newspaper Research Journal, 6*(1), 14.

Trayes, E. J. (1972). News/feature services by circulation group. *Journalism Quarterly, 49,* 133-137.

White, D. M. (1950). The "gatekeeper": A case study in the selection of news. *Journalism Quarterly, 22,* 383-390.

Whitney, C. D., & Becker, L. B. (1982). "Keeping the gates" for gatekeepers: The effects of wire news. *Journalism Quarterly, 59*(1), 60-65.

Wilhoit, G. C., & Sherrill, K. S. (1968). Wire service visibility of U.S. Senators. *Journalism Quarterly, 45,* 42-48.

Witcover, J. (1969). Washington: The workhorse wire services. *Columbia Journalism Review, 8,* 9-14.

Editorials' Influence

Bush, C. R. (Ed.). (1966, April). *News Research for Better Newspapers,* p. 104. 1:104. See also Vol. 2 (February 1967), p. 85.

Bush, C. R. (Ed.). (1967, February). *News Research for Better Newspapers,* p. 85.

Coombs, S. (1981). Editorial endorsements and electoral outcomes. In S. Coombs & M. B. MacKuen (Eds.), *More than news: Media power in public affairs.* Newbury Park, CA: Sage.

Counts, T. (1985). Effect of endorsements on presidential vote. *Journalism Quarterly, 62,* 644-647.

Fedler, F., Counts, T., & Stephens, L. F. (1982). Newspaper endorsements and voter behavior in the 1980 presidential election. *Newspaper Research Journal, 4*(1), 3.

Fedler, F., Smith, R. F., & Counts, T. (1985). Voter uses and perceptions of editorial endorsements. *Newspaper Research Journal, 6*(4), 19.

Gafke, R. A., & Leufhold, D. A. (1982, October 27). Why some editorial endorsements are more persuasive than others. *ANPA News Research Report No. 37.*

Hurd, R. E., & Singletary, M. W. (1984). Newspaper endorsement influence on the 1980 presidential election vote. *Journalism Quarterly, 61,* 332.

McCombs, M. (1967). Editorial endorsements: A study of influence. *Journalism Quarterly, 44*, 547.

Mueller, J. E. (1970). Choosing among 133 candidates. *Public Opinion Quarterly, 34*, 400.

Robinson, J. P. (1974). The press as king-maker: What surveys from last five campaigns show. *Journalism Quarterly, 51*, 591.

Rystrom, K. (1986). The impact of newspaper endorsements. *Newspaper Research Journal, 7*(2).

Shaw, D. (1977). *Journalism today: A changing press for a changing America* (pp. 72-86). New York: Harper's College Press.

St.Dizier, B. (1985). The effect of newspaper endorsements and party identification on voting choice. *Journalism Quarterly, 62*, 589-594.

Stempel, G. H., III. (1979, April). Types and topics of editorials in U.S. dailies. *Newspaper Research Journal* [Prototype], *3*.

Special Columns

Anderson, D. A. (1982). Examination of the content of the "Washington Merry-Go-Round." *Newspaper Research Journal, 3*(3), 45.

Bagdikian, B. J. (1964). How newspapers use columnists. *Columbia Journalism Review, 3*, 21, 24.

Bagdikian, B. J. (1966). How editors pick columnists. *Columbia Journalism Review, 5*, 41-42.

Himebaugh, G. A., & Kennedy, M. K. (1980). Book reviewing in the metropolitan press: A comparative study. *Newspaper Research Journal, 2*(1), 43.

Hynds, E. C. (1980). Kilpatrick, Anderson, Buchwald lead columnists into the 1980s. *Newspaper Research Journal, 2*(1), 19.

Wyatt, R. O., & Haskins, J. B. (1985). Book reviewing priorities in the American press: A survey. *Newspaper Research Journal, 6*(2), 8.

Teens' Content

ANPA News Research Center. (1969). Some newspaper content: 1952 and 1967. *News Research for Better Newspapers, 4*, 24-33.

Bogart, L. (1981). *Press and public: Who reads what, when, where, and why in American newspapers*. Hillsdale, NJ: Lawrence Erlbaum.

Campbell, L. R. (1971). Teenagers' readership of their hometown paper. In C. R. Bush (Ed.), *News Research for Better Newspapers, 5*, 108.

Carl J. Nelson Research. (1968). Profile of the teenage reader. In C. R. Bush (Ed.), *News Research for Better Newspapers, 3*, 71.

Davis, N. G., & Watkins, S. (1967). Teenage readers for Texas newspapers. In C. R. Bush (Ed.), *News Research for Better Newspapers, 2*, 42.

Lyle, J. (1968). The content of youth sections, pages and columns. *News Research for Better Newspapers, 3*, 95.

Times Dispatch and *News Leader* (Richmond, Virginia). (1967). Adult teenage readership compared. In C. R. Bush (Ed.), *News Research for Better Newspapers, 4*, 67-69.

Tribune (South Bend, Indiana). (1971). Readership of high school pages increases. In C. R. Bush (Ed.), *News Research for Better Newspapers, 5*, 75.

Cartoons and Comics

Brinkman, D. (1968). Do editorial cartoons and editorials change opinions? *Journalism Quarterly. 44*. 724-726.

Carl, L. M. (1968). Editorial cartoons fail to reach many readers. *Journalism Quarterly,* *44,* 533-535.

Davis, N. G., & Watkins, S. (1967). Teenage readers for Texas newspapers, 1961. In C. R. Bush (Ed.), *News Research for Better Newspapers, 2,* 42.

Dennis, E. E. (1974). The Regeneration of Political Cartooning. *Journalism Quarterly, 50,* 665-669.

Hynds, E. C. (1979, April). Herblock, Oliphant, MacNelly lead cartoon resurgence. *Newspaper Research Journal* [Prototype], *54.*

Milwaukee *Journal.* (1966). Sunday comics readership. In C. R. Bush (Ed.), *News Research for Better Newspapers, 1,* 37.

Riffe, D., Sneed, D., & Van Ommeren, R. L. (1985a). Behind the editorial page cartoon. *Journalism Quarterly, 62,* 378-383.

Riffe, D., Sneed, D., & Van Ommeren, R. L. (1985b). How editorial page editors and cartoonists see issues. *Journalism Quarterly, 62,* 896-899.

Robinson, E. J., & White, D. M. (1967). Comic strip reading in the United States. In C. R. Bush (Ed.), *News Research for Better Newspapers, 2,* 13.

Schramm, W., & White, D. (1949). Age, education, and economic status: Factors in newspaper reading. *Journalism Quarterly, 26,* 150-158.

Religion and Church Pages

Buddenbaum, J. M. (1982). News about religion: A readership study. *Newspaper Research Journal, 3*(2), 7.

Bogart, L. (1981). *Press and Public* (pp. 214-234). Hillsdale, NJ: Lawrence Erlbaum.

Rarick, G. (1967). Readership of the church page. In C. R. Bush (Ed.), *News Research for Better Newspapers, 2,* 34.

Root, R., & Bolder, H. (1966). The church page: Do readers like it? In C. R. Bush (Ed.), *News Research for Better Newspapers, 1,* 42.

Swain, B. M. (1982). Married Catholic priests: A case study of religion coverage. *Newspaper Research Journal, 3*(2), 18.

Public Relations' Contribution

Aronoff, C. E. (1976, Winter). Predictors of success in placing releases in newspapers. *Public Relations Review,* pp. 43-57.

Dunwoody, S., & Ryan, M. (1983). Public information persons as mediators between scientists and journalists. *Journalism Quarterly, 60,* 647-656.

Sachsman, D. B. (1976). Public relations influence on coverage of the environment in San Francisco area. *Journalism Quarterly, 53,* 54-60.

Stocking, S. H. (1985). Effect of public relations efforts on media visibility of organizations. *Journalism Quarterly, 62,* 358-366.

VanSlyke Turk, J. (1986). Information sources as media agenda-setters: A study of public relations' influence on the news. *Newspaper Research Journal, 7*(3).

3

WRITING AND EDITING

As the newsroom is the heart of the newspaper operation, research on writing and editing, content selection, and graphic display provides clues to improving reader interest in the product.

Analysis of writing and editing is one of the more fascinating aspects of newspaper research. The written product influences people's newspaper use, and this explains why the writing and editing process has received as much attention as any single aspect of newspapering. The research literature is vast. Consequently only selected areas of previous inquiry are discussed here. The first is writing.

READABILITY STUDIES

In the late 1940s, in conjunction with interest in students' reading attainment, a group of researchers devised formulas to estimate the reading difficulty of all forms of writing. Newspapers were quick to pay attention to any assessment of writing, and the formulas received wide attention in journalism writing classes—if not in the newsroom. The idea was that newspapers should be written to appeal to the widest general audience of readers. At that time it was believed a sixth grade reading level was the standard to approach. During the ensuing decades, dozens of studies attempted to assess the reading difficulty of a variety of newspaper content, and usually found, according to the formulas, newspapers were written at a twelfth grade or higher reading level. The possibility that newspapers were too difficult for the population to read was disturbing, particularly as readership research (Larkin, Grotta, & Stout, 1977) was indicating young people found newspapers difficult reading.

Newspaper hard news is more difficult reading than non-hard news content, and newspaper content generally is written at a reading level the average person might regard as difficult.

Hoskins (1973) found half the content of AP news and 83% of the content of UPI news in Texas either difficult or very difficult by the Flesch (1962) formula. Danielson and Bryan (1964) found wire service hard news more difficult to read than soft news, and Moznette and Rarick (1968) found editorials more readable than news stories in 10 West Coast dailies. Stempel (1981) studied six types of content in 21 newspapers. He determined international news was the most difficult to read, followed by local news and national news; but all six content categories were either difficult or very difficult reading by the Flesch formula. He said newspapers should be concerned about reader ability to handle the writing, based on the consistency of difficulty across content categories for all papers in the sample.

Readability formulas show newspapers are more difficult to read than popular novels and magazines, and this has been the case over time.

Fowler (1978; Fowler & Smith, 1979) found newspapers more difficult to read than best-selling novels and more difficult to read than popular magazines. While the newspapers sampled were easier to read in the study periods of 1904 and 1965 than they were in 1933, magazines had significantly greater readability in all three periods.

Virtually all the readability research on newspaper stories indicates:

A newspaper has everything to gain by insisting its news writers keep their sentence length in check.

An early study by American Press Institute (1954/1977) showed the ability of readers to understand a sentence dropped as the length of the sentence increased. While all members of their college-level sample could understand a sentence of six to eight words, only 47% could understand sentences of 30 words. Gunning (1952), Flesch (1962), and Berner (1983) all have recommended sentence length should average 20 words. Fusaro and Conover (1983) said a newspaper's purpose can be destroyed by writing that demands too much of a reader's skills. Burgoon, Burgoon, and Wilkinson (1981) said newspapers may have to lower their readability level to be effective.

While most of these researchers have used the readability formulas, recent investigations questioned the reliability of the readability formulas.

Readability formulas, which for 35 years have been used to gauge how difficult a story is to read, apparently are *not* consistent measures of reading difficulty.

Miller (1974) compared the Flesch formula and the Bormuth formula (a Cloze procedure that asks readers to fill in a deleted segment of a written passage) and found the Bormuth a more powerful predictor. But Miller questioned the ability of either formula to measure reading comprehension reliably.

Smith (1984) studied the three major readability formulas applied to newspapers. The Flesch formula, based on word and sentence length; the Gunning Fog Index, based on multisyllable "hard words"; and the Dale-Chall Formula, based on the number of "unfamiliar" words (those not on a list of 3,000 common words), were applied to national-international, state-local, and entertainment-feature stories in three newspapers. Results were that the three formulas differed in designating grade-level difficulties for newspaper content. While the Flesch scores were generally consistent with the Gunning scores, they indicated the newspaper content was about three grade levels more difficult than Dale-Chall scores showed. A related finding (Perera, 1980) showed the three formulas have difficulty measuring writing with subtle shades of meaning and with terse, condensed prose—exactly the kind of writing found in hard news articles. In all, these studies limit the applicability of current formulas to newspaper content assessment.

NEWSWRITING STYLE

While the newspaper industry is a multifaceted profession, most of its practitioners have more than a passing interest in and knowledge of the writing process. Virtually everyone associated with journalism has an appreciation of writing; so it follows that researchers have been enthralled with the topic as well.

Several recent studies have focused on aspects of newswriting that engage the reader's attention or make reading easier. One of the central themes has dealt with assessing if the inverted pyramid-5Ws writing style is superior to a narrative or more chronological writing style. Donohew, Palmgreen, and Duncan (1980) reported the reader's arousal level determines whether a story will be continued, and this occurs regardless of how the story gels with a reader's views. The researcher Donohew (1982) found: (1) narrative-style stories always produced more physiological arousal than the traditional summary-type stories; (2) narrative stories with direct quotes but passive verbs and adjectives were most arousing, those with direct quotes and active verbs and adjectives were next most arousing; (3) narrative, direct quote, active stories produced the most mood change; and (4) traditional summary, no direct quote, passive stories had the greatest decreases in arousal and the greatest negative mood change. Donohew noted that many newspaper stories are not breaking, hard-news stories and, given the flexibility nondeadline writing allows, reporters should consider using the narrative style more frequently.

Kerrick (1959) determined readers regarded the traditional 5W story treatment as stronger but more passive than the narrative. He concluded differences in writing style produced no differential attitude change for readers. Berner's (1983) limited study found little difference between the two writing styles or among headline-writing styles and suggested credibility would be no less for a narrative story than for the more traditional style. But the Kerrick and Berner studies form a minority report. Burgoon, Burgoon, and Wilkinson (1981) wrote, "The more colorful, dynamic and stimulating the writing style of the paper, the more frequently it is read, the more satisfied the reader and the higher the image." Cole and Shaw (1974) showed readers do notice powerful verbs and "body language." They find stories with such writing treatments brighter and the persons quoted more powerful and active. However, these styles caused readers, especially those who are more frequent newspaper readers, to view the entire news story with suspicion.

In a related study, Stapler (1985) looked at the sentence length in 360 staff-produced stories of 12 outstanding metropolitan newspapers. He found, "The 5W's lead, resulting in a one-sentence first paragraph, may defeat reading ease by making story openings more cumbersome reading." Stapler noted lead paragraphs, because they were twice as likely to be written in one sentence as later paragraphs, contained more words per sentence. Hence the leads were much more difficult to read than the rest of the news story. He advised that since this one-sentence-lead writing style is based on tradition and habit rather than logic, newspapers and wire services alike should consider the "one idea-one sentence" lead.

While Stapler's study considered the journalistic convention of writing one-sentence leads, other studies have dealt with stylistic considerations such as datelines and abbreviations. Shaw, Protzman, and Cole (1982) found datelines added little to reader knowledge. Smith and Voelz (1983) did a similar study of 383 college-level students and determined readers learned more about story location when the information was placed in the story rather than in a dateline. The wire service designation also was not understood or remembered by at least 30% of readers, regardless of whether it was a byline or in a dateline. Abbreviations such as "Sen." and "D-Minn." done according to journalistic style were not as well remembered or understood as they were when spelled, and using capitalized abbreviations of organizations was better understood than a generic designation of the organization in second references. Readers understood and remembered large numbers better as $1,500,000 than as $1.5 million. Finally, frequent newspaper readers were no more likely to understand or remember these journalistic styles than were infrequent readers. In all this study, like Stapler's, suggests reconsidering journalistic conventions in light of difficulties they may be causing readers.

Based on the Stapler and Smith studies:

> journalistic writing style conventions designed to produce stories efficiently or consistently, may be ignoring the key concern of reading ease.

Further evidence on the theme was provided by Weaver (1974), whose experiment found that readers judged stories no differently when one contained direct quotes and another only paraphrases. Also, readers' evaluation of persons in the stories did not differ on most measurements, although directly quoted persons were seen as more dramatic and more emotional. Finally the treatment of quotes had no demonstrable effect on reader comprehension or retention of factual material. The subjects in the experiment who were heavy newspaper readers found the direct quote articles less informative and less interesting; those who had considerable journalism experience scored lower on comprehension of the direct quote stories. The authors concluded conventional journalistic advice to use direct quotes is not necessarily designed with reader interest in mind. Culbertson and Somerick (1976) asked readers if they knew what quotes meant, and determined at least 85% knew. Readers were asked if they noticed bylines, and 70% said they usually or sometimes did. They thought bylines indicated the reporter was capable and was taking responsibility for writing the story, but they didn't link bylines with story importance. In fact, the lower educated and less politically knowledgeable were more likely to say bylines indicated story importance. And Culbertson and Somerick found that veiled attribution in news stories increased intrigue and reader interest, made sources seem knowledgeable, and did not adversely affect believability. So, here too, conventional journalistic wisdom is flawed if writers are being told to avoid using unnamed sources because such use lowers reader confidence in the story.

It must be noted that while journalistic writing styles may not maximize reader understanding, studies show:

> readers express no difficulties with the writing style of newspapers.

Bogart (1981) emphasizes that when the Newspaper Advertising Bureau asked women readers to appraise the writing style of the newspaper they were most familiar with, 83% described it as "about right for me." Likewise, few children who looked at newspapers considered the writing too difficult for them.

In other studies related to writing style, Ruffner and Burgoon (1981) used a standardized personality test (the Omnibus Personality Inventory) to see what effect personality has on journalists' writing styles. He reported the following relationships:

high tolerance for ambiguity and personal flexibility =	writing styles with more human interest
high social extroversion and low anxiety =	more punctuation in sentences; mature writing
less autonomous, more theoretical and higher intellectual disposition =	use more words per sentence (females use more words than males)
more complex, reserve their impulses, less altruism =	more adjectives, adverbs (females more emotive)
practical outlook, less intellectual disposition =	produce more readable message

Ruffner and Burgoon concluded personality types are better predictors of writing style than formal education, age, and sex, and personality may have a more enduring effect on writing style. They suggested there are implications for using personality measures to improve writing style both in journalism education and in the newsroom.

Smith (1980) looked at continuity in cumulative news stories over time and determined that even the New York *Times* contained little continuity of information in a given story set: 84% of the information in a continuing story appeared in only one article of the set. The researcher concluded newspapers make too little effort to fill in missing information for readers who might not have read all articles in a continuing news story.

In a study of whether people get more out of scientific stories when the stories contain parables, analogies, or examples, Grunig (1974) found story relevance to the reader's situation is a better predictor of understanding and involvement than the writing style. Readers who are problem solvers find parables most effective; analogies are second for problem solvers and even more effective for non-problem solvers; examples were less effective than straight story treatment. It is not known if these findings about writing style pertain to nonscientific writing.

Does writing apprehension affect the resulting story? Daly (1977) studied the written essays of 22 low apprehensives and 21 high apprehensives. He found those who didn't fear writing wrote significantly longer pieces. The unafraid used more words ending in *ly*, more commas, and more delimiting punctuation, although there was no significant difference in the use of uncommon or long words. There was no difference in the readability of writing by the two groups, but the quality of the writing was judged superior for the low apprehensives. Daly said those who aren't afraid to write probably have more writing experience, hence they are more elegant and expansive in their writing, but their writing is no more (or less) difficult to read. While this research suggests virtually all would-be journalists will be free of writing apprehension, it does support the notion that more writing background equates to better writing.

One recent researcher (Pitts, 1982) used a simple and innovative strategy to determine how reporters write their stories. She asked them to talk aloud into a tape recorder while they wrote their copy. She found the three pros composed the lead—often more than one paragraph—first and spent one-fourth to one-third of their entire writing time on the lead because they said they considered it the most important aspect of the story. Stories were written in sequences: first reviewing notes, then planning and writing the lead, writing the story, then rereading and editing it. Stories were written in small units, one at a time, and these were often edited as they were being written through a recursive process. Story organization was not planned in advance, and no preevaluations of story quality were made. There was no ordering of facts by importance. Instead, each sentence or paragraph was worked individually as the writer completed the task at hand without considering the overall effect. Writers frequently used recall to recreate dialogue, to regain information from memory, and to lead them back to their notes. Few sentences were planned, although the beginning of the sentence might be with the rest following as the writer typed. Editing occurred at every phase of the writing process as these reporters clarified, rewrote, or added while writing. They reread only one or two sentences at a time while writing. Editing that occurred after the story was written involved rereading the entire story, polishing grammar, and correcting punctuation and spelling. Although interruptions occurred continually while they were writing, the writing process continued without extensive rereading.

Among insights offered by the Pitts study are: (1) leads are important as more than attention getters—they help organize the newswriting process; (2) newswriters don't follow a sequence of planning, outlining, and rewriting—they don't even rank-order facts; (3) continuing paragraph ideas follow from paragraphs just written; (4) stories are written by the sentence and paragraph; (5) editing is an integral part of the writing process rather than an after-the-fact activity; (6) recall, notes, rereading, judgment, and general knowledge provide the fodder for writing, but memory was the most important tool used; (7) having gathered the information was critical to recall in the writing process and news gathering was closely linked with newswriting; (8) writing and thinking were simultaneous and mutually supportive; (9) newswriters are able to keep writing through distractions; and (10) confidence in their writing ability and decision making was necessary for successful newswriting.

And perhaps the most important insight gained from the Pitts study is that a straightforward and innovative research strategy can yield such a wealth of information about the newswriting process. The industry and academic researchers alike would do well to continue along these lines in future projects on newswriting styles.

DECISION MAKING BY EDITORS

The research literature is replete with studies about newspaper editing, editors, and design strategies. There is so much, in fact, that the most narrow definition of the editing process—the editor's content decision making—will have to suffice here. Attention can be paid only to the key studies.

The theoretical basis for studying news editing is the gatekeeping (White, 1950) process: Editors are viewed as the primary news flow "gates" with the opportunity of initiating the news flow by making story assignments, stopping the news flow, altering the news story along its path to publication, or allowing the news flow to continue without interference. We know editor gatekeepers work within the constraints of time, space, resource availability, personal biases, their news value definitions, the newsroom organizational structure, their backgrounds and educational influences, the larger organizational constraints related to their newspaper's ownership, their management styles, and influences associated with the journalistic world beyond their newsrooms. News editors are depicted as having the most difficult job in journalism.

Newswriters are also sensitive to newsroom pressure. Gieber (1960) found reporters reacted to contraints such as deadlines, understaffing, newshole space availability, newspaper policy and climate, and the freedom they had to follow a story. Instead of thinking about the reading public when writing a story, reporters often have the editor or fellow newspersons in mind.

> The internal newsroom or newspaper situation, the learned tenets of journalism and selected practices of the profession have more influence on the content newspapers publish than do most external factors.

The news-editing process may be compared with a hospital's operating room. Medical staff perform as a team of specialists, each of whom is under time and resource constraints, greatly concerned about meeting performance expectations of coworkers, conscious of meeting prescribed standards of the hospital, mindful of the required bureaucratic procedures of record keeping, aware of medical protocol, and responding to their own training and experience levels. The environment is designed to ensure meeting minimum standards of patient care, but the care and comfort of the patient can become a secondary consideration compared with getting the job done according to accepted procedures. Likewise, while informing the public is considered the primary goal of newspapers, the day-to-day activities of the news-processing environment often relegate that objective to a secondary consideration.

The classic study on newsroom socialization and the constraints that influence news flow from reporting through publication was Breed's (1955) investigation of newsroom practices. He concluded a wide variety of organizational constraints leads to homogeneity of news handling, particularly among the more "socialized" staffers. Donohew (1967) found publisher attitude on a news topic was more predictive of coverage than the community condition or perceived community opinion. Olien, Donohue, and Tichenor (1968) concluded that a newspaper with a powerful publisher is less likely to report news of conflict and controversy. Bowers (1967) studied managing editors at 613 evening dailies and found publishers were active in news selection when: (1) the story is geographically close; (2) the story is likely to affect newspaper revenues; (3) the publisher is personally involved; (4) the paper is smaller; and (5) the decision is *not* to use a story. Edelstein (1966) noted the homogeneity of news and controls resulting from newsroom organization mediate change and protect the public from disruptive pressures. He wrote, "The media are guarantors that a body of common ultimate values remains viable as a continuing source of consensus, despite the inroads of change."

Lippmann was quoted as writing:

> Every newspaper when it reaches the reader is the result of a whole series of selections as to what items shall be printed, in what position they shall

be printed, how much space each shall occupy, which emphasis each shall have. There are no objective standards here. There are only conventions (1966: 150).

Although news values are taught in journalism schools and are learned on the job in the newsroom, many studies have noted the lack of reliance on the same news values in making editorial decisions about stories. Singletary (1977) provided an overview of research on news values that enumerated the constraints on the selection and editing of news. Still, definitive conclusions could not be reached.

> While it appears there is no explicit or pervasively accepted pattern of news value importance, there is a standardization of media news values used.

Sasser and Russell (1972) found that although all media in a metropolitan area carried the same prominent stories, the lack of overlap beyond these few stories indicated news editors lacked consistency in news judgment. Breed (1955) showed that understaffing and lack of standardized news judgment caused editors to adopt an "arterial" flow of news selection: smaller newspapers took their agenda of news selection from decisions made by the wire services and larger papers. Gieber (1956) found a similar occurrence among wire editors who were overwhelmed with the mechanical details of production and who therefore relied on the wire service news budgets for news selection. Gieber said these wire editors were passive gatekeepers with nebulous news values. They viewed the public as stereotyped special interest groups. Shaw (1969) noted news editors' nonvalue technological constraints (newshole space available) resulted in a close relationship between wire news received and that published. He concluded the wire services play an important role in determining what will be news in a given day. Lindeborg and Stone (1974) compared news content in a sample of New York newspapers in 1950 and 1970 and found none of the 15 categories of general news changed more than 4% during the 20-year span.

> Although there may be little standardization in news values, there is great standardization both in media decisions of which events will be covered and in how the media report events.

This finding has been reached by virtually all research studies that assessed actual media content. It is one of the central themes supporting the theory of agenda setting, as McCombs and Shaw (1972) wrote:

the high correlations . . . suggest consensus on news values, especially on major news items. Although there is no explicit, commonly agreed-upon definition of news, there is a professional norm regarding major news stories from day to day. These major-story norms doubtless are greatly influenced by widespread use of major wire services—especially by newspapers and television—for much political information.

Much of the accumulated information on content decisions is summarized in Gaye Tuchman's *Making News* (1978). Reporting findings of other researchers as well as her own, Tuchman offers some points worth remembering:

- The balance of news appearing in newspapers represents ongoing "editorial negotiation," the give-and-take of editors who must work in the same bureaucratic organization (the newspaper) every day. Negotiation permits a news output that reflects the news input of reporters and wire services. This negotiation represents a purposive attempt to allow news to pass through the gates in the same proportion at which it enters. (31-38)

- Mechanical constraints, including available time, require a routine for making content decisions. This routine will be altered only for highly newsworthy and unpredictable occurrences. When such events happen, news "professionalism" comes into play because personnel are capable of putting the routine aside to cope with the unexpected. (58-62)

- The construction of reality presented by the news media is based on content decision makers' understanding of the society. While this view of reality is open to change, it is also dependent on journalistic conventions of what constitutes news. News values are learned from being in the profession. (182-196)

Other researchers have suggested the paramount news value is impact. Atwood (1970) found that while desk-bound editors were least likely to predict story preferences of readers, other newspersons did agree with readers in finding impact the most preferred news element; conflict was second. Buckalew's (1969) study of television news editors showed the high impact stories were greatly favored, particularly if they contained video. Clyde (1969) found newspaper and broadcast editors' news selections were similar and both based selection on conflict first, proximity second, and timeliness third. Ward (1967) found that high-impact news was valued most by city editors, followed by oddity, prominence of the individuals involved, conflict, and consequence.

ELECTRONIC EDITING

More relevant to daily editing activities in the newsroom is the recent research on changes in writing-editing practices that have come about through use of video display terminals (VDTs). Early discussion of the new electronic devices concerned the type of hardware, its adoption rate by the industry, and its acceptance by newsroom personnel. Only since the 1980s has there been any significant research into how VDTs have changed the news-editing process.

At first, inquiries indicated VDTs were slower than the former pencil editing procedures used for years. Fisher (1978) said editors perceived greater speed and higher quality on the machines, but found actual time spent editing was longer, a finding Crook (1977) derived as well. Bennett (1977), Kurtz (1980), and Wolton (1979) found problems with the system ranging from slower speeds to fear of upsetting the traditional organizational structure of the newsroom.

> But studies finding serious fault with the electronic editing systems were done during the system's experimental stages. The bulk of studies confirm VDTs are superior editing devices.

Doebler (1974) and others wrote that the new systems were more error-free, faster, and allowed later deadlines. Stulce (1976) found the systems reduced typographical and grammar errors and increased editor efficiency. Lindley (1977) said VDTs give the copy editor more autonomy and allow editors to make more extensive changes in all copy, including wire copy. Randall (1979) analyzed the Charlotte (North Carolina) *Observer* before and after a VDT system had been installed and reported fewer errors in spelling, punctuation, sentence construction, hyphenation, and typography, although the average sentence length remained the same. Shipley (1979) said most editors liked working with VDTs, and editors with a positive attitude toward the machines worked faster.

Garrison (1982; see also Garrison, 1980) studied four years of news copy at the Milwaukee *Journal*, two years of copy prior to the installation of VDTs and two after. He found most copydesk editor time was devoted to editing text material followed by time writing headlines. In handling wire copy, the editor spent most time cutting stories (from an average of 255 words provided to 44 words published), and usually cut wire stories from the bottom up, although this wasn't always the case. The editor cut paragraphs and sentences from wire stories, frequently changed copy to conform to the local paper's style, but rarely reorganized wire stories. As deadlines neared, more time was spent writing heads and editing late stories. Almost all of the changes in copy were made by the slot editors, the first gate for wire news. Half of the editors using the VDT system said electronic editing had no effect on decision making. Among negative effects were fear of the new technology and the belief it slowed the editing process. Positive effects mentioned were that the system speeded the process and allowed greater flexibility and experimentation on deadline. Editors said they edited more carefully since they (instead of the composing room personnel) were now the last to see the copy.

Garrison's editors had trouble conceptualizing story length on the screens, and they used the VDT system's count keys frequently. All agreed headline writing on the machines was vastly superior to the pencil-and-paper procedure used previously. They used the VDTs head-count button, tried more word substitutions in head writing, and believed the machines led to better-fitting heads. Having the system did not increase the number of wire stories that received local information inserts, and editors did not believe the machines affected their news judgment. There was almost unanimous agreement that accuracy had been improved with the system, but editors said speed was a push: While much of the actual editing was faster, editors' increased responsibility of being the last to process copy took longer. But Garrison concluded that an electronic editing system designed to match the nonelectronic editing tasks it would replace could be accepted in the newsroom easily and without altering editors' decision making.

The potential health hazard of VDTs has been another area of debate and recent research. Sneed (1985) summarized the topic and determined, "So far, no causal link between VDT radiation exposure and human health problems has been established," but he noted allegations of injury do exist. Presenting an overview of the main arguments for and against VDT legislation, Sneed said the newspaper industry—definitely a combatant in the issue—has provided little opportunity for airing the pros or cons in print.

A more recent phase of new technology in newsrooms and in newspaper libraries is subscribing to data bases—Nexis, Dialog, VuText, Dow Jones News/Retrieval, and so forth—for backgrounding stories, checking accuracy, and adding information in current news reports. Data bases are electronically distributed indexes and text of periodical reports that augment the traditional newspaper morgue. Ullmann (1983) encouraged data base use by investigative reporters and others. He surveyed 100,000-plus circulation newspapers and found 20 of the 54 papers that replied subscribed to one or more data bases, although most of the respondents were librarians. He described how the bases were being used and how they could be used successfully for searches. McDonald (1984) got replies from 39 of 41 dailies (mostly in the 300,000- to 400,000-circulation category) using the data bases and described how they were being used by newspaper librarians. Endres (1985) did the first survey of all circulation levels of newspapers to determine the extent of data base use. He confirmed that larger-circulation papers were the most likely users, primarily papers with circulations over 100,000. Endres reported 21 papers in his sample were using data bases: 15 used only one service; 4 used two services; and 2 used five services. Nexis, the most extensive information provider, was the chief service used. Most of the papers had used the services for a year or less at the time of the survey, and because of costs, only 6 subscribed to the complete package of full text, abstracts, and indexes. But it was evident from responses that the data bases were well liked. Endres found that papers not using the data bases, although interested in them, didn't know much about them. Editors who were familiar with them but didn't use them said cost precluded subscribing.

Data bases were being used for business information, information about individuals, and information about political events. Respondents said the data bases' greatest contribution was general background on persons, events, or companies; and the data bases were used for in-depth articles, investigative pieces, spot news, features, analyses, and editorials, in that order. Users were general assignment reporters and management-level editors; investigative reporters, business, feature, and political writers, in that order. Endres found librarians were usually in charge of the system, or on papers without a librarian, a "systems editor" was the overseer. Librarians who controlled access to the system said reporters were not specific enough in their requests for information. Some had become so reliant on the system that they wouldn't begin to write a story without a search. News editors were mixed in their view of the system's worth.

The research seems to assure:

> data bases to support the newswriting and editing functions are likely to be the next major technological advance for newspapers. Their use will bring greater efficiency, accuracy, and comprehensiveness to the newsroom operation and to news stories. Data bases are likely to be an accepted newsroom resource by 1990.

Along with the studies already mentioned, Miller (1983) and Ruth (1985) reported the advantages and acceptance of data bases in the newsroom. The relationship between the newsroom's use of information and that of a library was discussed by Ward and Hansen (1986), who saw many similarities between the two—in spite of the major differences each profession might extoll. They predicted that when newspapers have developed full-text storage and retrieval of their own library files, they will use electronic data bases simultaneously. And Ward and Hansen looked beyond the current acceptance levels toward fundamental changes that data base access might bring to the writing and editing process.

WHAT TO DROP AND WHAT TO KEEP

We may assume proprietary research has done much in the area of newspaper management choices on what content to drop and what to keep. However, the public domain literature has included tips on this decision-making process only in the last 10 years. With increased competition for available news space, the desire to keep current readers, and the need to attract new ones, editors are anxious to make every column inch of newshole perform its maximum reader-attraction function. The available research centers on evaluating strategies for decision making rather than attempting actually to decide among items of newspaper content. Hence, the advice provided is suitable for adoption in a variety of market situations.

Mauro (1977) offers some general advice about readership of newspaper content items. Although the study was in one market on a relatively small sample, its findings are similar to those of hundreds of self-reported readership studies across the country, on larger samples and over time. In short, the findings offered in Table 3.1 are worth remembering about newspaper readership generally.

Adult readers, regardless of their sex or age, do find the hard news portions of the newspaper interesting. About 40% of their reading activity is in the hard news cluster of items, including human-interest stories and topics of social concern. Another 17% of their reading activity is devoted to sports, and this is true for both sexes. Next comes entertainment, getting about 10% of total reading activity. Finally, business listings and general service such as weather and obituaries 6%. Admittedly, the figures offered are in percentages of total reading activity, and while many people read the weather and obituaries every day, we wouldn't expect single items of content to take a great bite of total reading activity even if they are very high in readership. The figures are presented to reinforce research findings that consistently show

TABLE 3.1

Broad Content Areas of Interest to Male and
Female Readers, All Adult Ages

Item Set	Males	Females
Hard news content including business stories, crime and accident stories, local, state, national, and international government, human interest, military and war stories, topics of social concern (consumer, and so on)	41%	41%
Local, regional, national and international sports, sports listings	16%	18%
Humor and entertainment (comics, and so on), serialized comic strips	9%	11%
Business listings, general service (weather, obits, and so on)	6%	6%

NOTE: From "Readers' Reaction to Newspaper Design" by C. Bain & D. Weaver, 1979, *Newspaper Research Journal, 1,* Copyright 1982 by Newspaper Research Journal. Reprinted by permission.

readers devote more reading activity to hard news. With that in mind, strategies of content retention or deletion can be offered.

McCombs (1977) described how comics or other regularly run newspaper features can be selected. He noted two pieces of information are necessary to make the what-to-drop, what-to-keep decision: (1) the proportion of the audience actually reading a content item every time it appears—those who regularly, occasionally, or never read each item— and (2) a measure of how each feature is clustered with others—do people who generally read one kind of content also read similar content in the cluster? McCombs says the first piece of information can be derived from any reliable readership study while the second is determined by factor analysis of the content items' readership. Some features will be clustered with others; some will stand alone.

> Look for features with low readership which are clustered with other content in the newspaper. These are the likely candidates for deletion.

The pattern emerging from combining the two pieces of information appears in Figure 3.1. The optimal features for retaining are those that have high readership and are isolated from others, block A. Many

A	C
High Readership but Isolated	Low Readership and Isolated
B	D
High Readership and Clustered	Low Readership and Clustered

Figure 3.1 Typology of Newspaper Content in the Decision of What to Drop and What to Keep (NOTE: From "What to Drop and What to Keep" by M. E. McCombs, 1977, *ANPA News Research Report No. 4*. Copyright 1977 by ANPA. Reprinted by permission.)

readers follow these items intensely, and the paper would be offering no direct content substitute for such readers if the items were dropped. Block D features also should be retained because, while they aren't being read by many, those who do read them would not have another item to substitute. Block B items should be dropped with caution. There are other substitutes being offered, but these features do have high readership and dropping them would be chancy. The block C features are the prime candidates for deletion because they get low readership and there are substitutes to which these readers can turn. McCombs suggested identifying block C features will end an editor's deletion problems because there will be enough such items in the newspaper to solve most space needs. He used one-third of the readers being frequent item readers as a cutting point, with items getting that much readership earmarked as high and those with less earmarked as low. But McCombs cautioned not all block C features could be deleted since some would be in the same clusters.

Meyer (1979) looked at comic strips as perhaps the single continuing what-to-drop, what-to-keep problem. He pointed out that basing the decision merely on deleting those with the lowest total readership might lose some readers who follow the strips intensely or might lose some portions of the reading audience the newspaper particularly wants to retain. Meyer's research began with a factor-analysis clustering of the strips by readers' rating of readership on a 7-point scale. The outcome was three clusters of comic strips under the headings of dramatic serial, sophisticated humor, and light humor; and each group drew a somewhat different type of reader. Meyer then offered some decision models for determining which comics to delete:

(1) Drop the strip with the smallest number of readers, although there is a great risk that some deletions will actually lose newspaper subscribers.
(2) Drop the strips with the least reader intensity interest levels.
(3) Use proportional representation based on the three groups of comics. Here the number of comics per group would be kept in proportion to readers of that group, dropping first the least read.
(4) Create a scale combining readership and reading intensity, and drop those on the bottom rungs of the scale.
(5) Use the McCombs typology of readership versus isolation clustering.
(6) Use a "Max 4" model, which is based on knowing that the majority of readers give four comics maximum ratings; so deleting occurs for those strips with the least reduction in the number of people who still give four comics a maximum rating.
(7) Watch for a bimodal distribution which might occur for controversial comics, in which case some readers would like them greatly and others would not read them at all. It might be important to keep these for those who read them intensely.

Decision-making models seem complicated. Indeed, Meyer (1978) discussed the problem of using the more sophisticated models and suggested editors consider a "pragmatic middle ground" by using editorial prioritization. The model uses the two measures of readership and clustering, but adds a new wrinkle: Is the content associated with newspaper reading? If interest is high and readers do not currently associate the topic with newspapers, the item is a likely candidate for developing new reader interest.

Subber and Schweitzer (1980) described a relatively inexpensive and novel method of determining which comics to keep. Involving readers in the decision, the paper published an in-paper poll of comic strips with choices. A small-sample reader survey was done as well as a check on the in-paper poll. Readers were asked to check each of the comics usually read and to indicate which two were enjoyed most and least. The survey was carrier-delivered and its findings were similar to those of the poll on the key comic interest items (although, predictably, both mail-in procedures overrepresented people who were avid readers of comics). Subber and Schweitzer admitted the procedures were less precise than a random study, but found that combining the measures of readership and like-dislike provided a referendum and cluster matrix similar to those recommended by McCombs and Meyer.

It should not be thought the what-to-drop, what-to-keep solutions are good only for decisions about comics. McCombs's approach to the topic is designed to be applied to all newspaper content, and Meyer (1985) discussed a research project on subscription price increase and retention patterns that found the mix of editorial content was the chief predictor of subscriber retention.

THE NEWSHOLE AND ITS CONTENT

What does the newspaper contain, and how consistent is its content mix over time? Research provides many answers, although the methods of tabulation vary greatly. In fact, one of the major problems limiting knowledge about newspaper content is the variety of approaches research studies have taken, depending on the investigator's intent.

For instance, the broadest possible division of newspaper content would be distinguishing all news and editorial content from all advertising content. Next, news content might be differentiated from opinion content. News content could further be divided into "hard" versus "soft" news (a procedure that has been used, although the distinction is often fuzzy—is the personality profile sidebar on the newly elected city council member a hard or a soft news item?). Many studies have investigated only hard news, but the category breakdowns might be international, national, state, local, and so forth. Other approaches have involved distinctions such as government, education, crime, disaster, science, and so forth. Still other approaches have focused on more subtle content differences such as terrorism versus more general crime or airplane hijackings versus other airplane disasters.

The point is that it's nearly impossible to synthesize content decision research because the variety of approaches has been so great. The best that can be attempted here is to view some of the findings of research that took similar approaches: distinctions among relatively broad news and feature content categories into which large blocks of newspaper content can be classified. Stone (1975) provided a content breakdown by publication frequency for newspapers with circulations under 8,000. The figures were compiled in terms of content costs, with each category indicating a different level of cost investment by newspapers in the sample (see Table 3.2).

The study found that content carried was related to publication frequency; for instance, weeklies carried an average of 2.5% wire news, semi-weeklies an average 6%, and small dailies about 10%. Further,

TABLE 3.2

Percentages of Cost Content Categories for

Newspapers with Circulation under 8,000

Category	Weeklies	Semiweeklies	Dailies	All
Wire news	2.5	6.0	10.3	8.6
Local news	7.1	5.9	5.4	6.7
Local society and sports	5.1	5.3	4.9	5.0
Syndicated features	2.8	2.5	8.0	4.6
Public relations sources	5.2	4.2	3.0	4.6
Editorials and columns	2.1	2.3	2.0	2.1
Nonstaff correspondents	6.5	4.7	2.7	5.5
Obituaries	1.3	1.5	1.1	1.2
Miscellaneous items	3.2	1.5	1.7	2.7
Headline and white space	10.5	12.4	12.4	11.0
Wire pictures	1.5[a]	—[a]	2.4	2.3
Local pictures	5.2	5.8	4.6	5.1
Free pictures	2.5	3.0	1.6	2.3
National ads	14.2	15.8	15.1	14.7
Local ads	26.6	25.5	21.4	25.2
Classified ads	6.8	8.6	7.4	7.1
Legal ads	4.7	3.8	2.2	4.2
Political ads	6.8	6.4	3.7	6.1

a. Responses below 20% for these categories.

there were virtually no differences in content for group-owned newspapers or those individually owned.

Lindeborg and Stone (1974) offered the more usual approach to category compilation in a sample of six New York state newspapers' front pages in 1950 and 1970 (see Table 3.3). The principle finding of the comparison was the remarkable similarity of content contained on front pages during the 20-year period: none of the categories varied by more than 4%. This was true in spite of the changes in American society and the substantial increase in the number of newspaper pages during the study's time span.

The Newspaper Advertising Bureau, Inc. (1978) provided figures on content carried by a sample of dailies in 1971 and 1977 (see Table 3.4). While the NAB figures were taken from newspapers with vastly different circulation sizes—papers with 100 pages would be offering *more* news in each of the content categories than papers with only 50 pages—a comparison (not shown) by circulation sizes revealed the proportion of content by category was substantially the same.

Hard news is the major bill of fare in daily newspapers, and while frequency of publication may influence the cost source of news, newspaper size makes little difference in the proportion of news carried. Also,

TABLE 3.3
Subject Matter of Front-Page Stories in
Six Upstate New York Papers (in percentages)

Topic	1950	1970	Topic	1950	1970
Military	16	18	Weather	4	3
Government	12	14	Public morals	1	3
Disasters	15	11	Health and welfare	1	3
Politics	10	14	Education/arts	1	2
Crime	8	12	Popular amusements	3	1
Human interest	6	7	Science/invention	1	—
Labor and unions	6	4	Miscellaneous	10	5
Economics	6	3			

NOTE: From "News Values as Reflected in Newspaper Content Found Stable from 1950 Through 1970" by R. Lindeborg & G. C. Stone, 1974, *Research for Better Newspaper, 7,* Copyright 1974 by ANPA. Reprinted by permission.

TABLE 3.4
News and Editorial Content, Longer than Five Inches,
in American Dailies, 1971 and 1977

	All Sampled Dailies	
	1971	1977
General Interest	66.8%	66.6%
Local and State News	12.7	12.4
International News	10.2	6.3
U.S. Government, Domestic	6.9	3.5
Other General Interest	37.0	44.4
Sports	14.2	13.9
Business and Finance	6.9	7.3
Fashion, Society, Food, Home, Garden, etc.	5.4	3.3
Columns	5.3	3.9
Other Items	1.4	5.0

NOTE: From "Two Dimensions of News: Interest and Importance Ratings of the Editorial Content of the American Press," 1978. Copyright 1978 by ANPA. Reprinted by permission.

the indication is that the proportion of news content available to readers remains relatively stable over time.

Do newspaper editors recognize the breakdown of content their papers carry? One study (Drew & Wilhoit, 1976) indicated they may not. Asked to estimate the news space devoted to various news content, a sample of 149 managing editors said 75% of total newshole was devoted to local news. Other estimates included: sports, 6%; national, 4%;

women's, 4%; international, 3%; editorial, 3%; state, 3%; and financial, 2%. While most editors said they were satisfied with the available space, obviously their estimates of the categories for local, state, national, and international news differ greatly from the actual content being published in newspapers, according to the NAB figures compiled about the same time. The comparison between fact and perception suggests editors aren't as familiar with the documented research as they should be.

GRAPHIC DESIGN AND PACKAGING

If the extensive body of research literature is any indication, it's easier (or more interesting) to study graphic design than to probe into story content of newspapers. Graphics studies are legion. They encompass virtually every aspect of newspaper design: body type, headlines, columns, photos, cutlines, page layout, white space, boxes, indexes, section fronts, color, and the smearing properties of inks. The major problem with this research is that it becomes quickly dated. As new findings and fads set the trends that will be followed, the older inquiries lose favor and seem almost foolish. For instance, a major controversy in the 1950s concerned the readability of serif versus sans-serif type. The research outcome favored sans serif and today few papers use the more traditional serif type. Other graphics changes have occurred in a similar manner, although evolution rather than revolution governs the newspaper design field. Design changes are likely to be adopted along a normal curve with a very few innovators initiating a practice, a few more early adopters trying the concept, then the majority making the change, and—of course—laggards who simply refuse to give up their comfortable, customary ways.

The approach here will be from the broadest to the narrowest aspect of graphic design, beginning with adoption of modern newspaper design practices.

Adoption of Modern Design

By definition, *modern design* means horizontal or modular makeup of a page. However, the term has come to include as well those design changes advocated about the same time as modular makeup including, but not limited to, no column rules, six-column format, use of boxes, down-style heads, modern Roman type, and white space around heads.

By the mid-1980s, newspapers were expected to have completed their 10-year trend of adopting modern graphic design. Evidence indicated adopting the new design was a calculated effort to modernize newspapers generally, based on research findings about reader preferences.

Click and Stempel (1979) replicated a 1973 study of the adoption of modern design practices and found in a national sample that adoption was well under way by both larger and smaller dailies. Front pages were treated differently from inside pages, as the inside pages were less likely to show modern designs consistently. Some 80% of the larger papers were using six-column format on inside pages compared with only about 40% of the smaller papers, and smaller papers were less likely to break up body type on inside pages.

The one characteristic of modern format not found in wide use in 1978 was four-color pictures: Only 21% of large dailies and 4% of smaller dailies used a color picture in the five days of editions analyzed. A total of 35% of the papers used tint blocks, color borders, nameplates, or other form of color on page one; but the front page was likely to be the only one in the paper that contained any color. While Click and Stempel found uneven adoption of all aspects of modern design, compared with what newspapers were doing in 1972-1973 (Weaver, Mullins, & McCombs, 1974) and their own study in 1967, they concluded the industry had come a long way toward adopting modern design. They tested whether adoption of modern design was related to circulation increases over a 10-year period, but found no relationship.

Weaver, Mullins, and McCombs (1974) compared content and appearance of market leaders and trailers (by circulation) in 23 cities. Findings showed trailers used more modern design, and there was no indication modern design was associated with increased circulation. The study did find some patterns reversed among the largest dailies and those in the north-central region.

Utt and Pasternak (1984) did an analysis of editor responses to a survey about their design practices. Findings showed most American newspapers had adopted modern design and that editors thought pleasing graphic design offered them a competitive edge. Those who used modular design were most satisfied with the appearance of their papers. Utt and Pasternak said newspapers were graphically similar before 1965, went through a period of dissimilarity during the next 15 years as some went to the modern design and some did not, and by 1980 were again graphically similar since most had adopted the modern design.

Stone, Schweitzer, and Weaver (1978) used a national sample of jointly owned morning-evening dailies (all free from real competitive situations) to determine if adoption of modern newspaper design was related to circulation size, to having more sections, or to the paper's geographic location. Describing this mid-1970s state of graphic use, their study showed papers generally were using longer and deeper headlines, were using boxes around some stories, but were not using color with pictures or graphic variety in story-body type. Other findings indicated modern newspaper design was not being adopted quickly by Northeastern papers. Instead, those in the Southeast, Southwest, and on the West Coast were moving most rapidly toward modern design. Smaller papers were slightly more likely than large papers to use modern design. Significant relationships were found between adopting modern design and papers with a higher percentage of street sales and greater city zone circulation. The implication was that metropolitan area papers were using modern design, and the graphic tactic was used to attract single-copy buyers. The authors tested for a correlation between modern design and "sensational" design (e.g., screaming banner heads), but found no such relationship existed.

Weaver (1977) compared how sister newspapers' appearance might affect their audience penetration. He found if the number of columns on page one was different, both newspapers were likely to have high audience penetration. Since number of page-one columns was the only difference noted, he concluded similar appearance by sister papers is associated with higher penetration, but cautioned there may not be any cause-and-effect relationship. Using the same data base of jointly owned morning-evening papers, Schweitzer, Weaver, and Stone (1977) reported that in such ownership situations the look-alike pairs have a slight tendency to reach a higher percentage of two-newspaper households.

A more recent investigation of the possible link between modern graphic design use and newspaper competition (Utt & Pasternak, 1985) was done on separately owned 100,000-plus circulation newspapers in 10 cities. They found pairs of competing newspapers in a close circulation battle tended to be more similar in appearance than those for which the circulation gap was wide. Circulation trailers used more modern design, papers with the highest circulations used more traditional design, and morning papers used more modern design. They concluded that in the nation's largest competitive newspaper markets there is a trend toward conformity of appearance, and "Generally, as the competition increases, so does the sameness."

The use of modern graphic design can be examined in terms of its appeal to readers.

Virtually all recent studies of modern design indicate readers prefer it. Some studies show it takes awhile for readers to get used to the graphic changes in their familiar local paper, but readers will normally agree within three months that the change is a welcome improvement.

Click and Stempel (1982) tested reader preferences for modular design through a three-market study of newspaper front pages selected to provide a variety of color and makeup possibilities. The two modular pages with color finished first and second in all three markets, and most results supported reader preference for color and modern design except a spot-color, modular paper that finished last in all three cities. The authors speculated there are factors other than color and modular design that might account for reader preference, but believed the study confirmed newspapers using modular design and color were on the right track.

Garcia, Click, and Stempel (1981) found changes made by a newspaper's design team were immediately recognized and accepted by readers. Three weeks later, the preference was even more favorable. Schweitzer's experiment on front pages (1980) showed readers preferred the modern design and liked boxes on page one with references to inside stories. They particularly liked boxes of page-one news summaries. The researcher recommended editors use such summaries to keep the news story count on page one high, a balance against the lower story count with modern graphic design.

Other Graphic Considerations

Bain and Weaver (1979) did a series of experiments and a field study of jumps, wraps, and type styles. Findings about jumps were that the more stories on page one (more stories are supposed to be a greater reader-interest draw), the less space can be devoted to pictures and the more page-one stories will have to be jumped inside the paper. Readers hate jumped stories and do not generally follow them to the inside; so the recommendation was to keep the number of jumps to a minimum. Findings on wraps were that readers prefer the straight and not-so-narrow layout to raw wraps or doglegs. "Columns with equal depth seem to be quicker and easier to navigate," the researchers said. However, they pointed out readers can follow the uneven wraps. Findings on headlines were that size of type, rather than weight or slant, indicated story importance to readers. While readers weren't able to discern hard news from features based on whether headline type was Roman or italic, the researchers concluded these type styles might be used at the editor's discretion without adverse effect on readers.

Some Photo Findings

Pictures have increased readers' enjoyment and interest in newspapers since these graphic images could be reproduced on newsprint. Research on photos consistently supports the following:

(1) People like pictures, especially those in full color, and people's attention is arrested more by pictures than by stories.

(2) While pictures are themselves among the most highly regarded newspaper content, they lend interest to stories, captions, and headlines (Baxter, Quarles, & Kosak, 1978). So pictures complement rather than compete with associated newspaper content. Larger photographs draw more attention than smaller ones (Rarick, 1967), and pictures related to a story draw more attention to the associated story.

(3) Certain types of pictures are more effective reader draws than other types, but it is unclear which types of pictures are the best reader draws (Wolf, 1985).

(4) Color picture use by *USA Today* may influence the future treatment of pictures in most American newspapers as it has been the acknowledged trend-setter in graphics since its inception (Geraci, 1983).

REFERENCES

Readability Studies

American Press Institute. (1977). In M. Ryan & J. W. Tankard, Jr. (Eds.), *Basic News Reporting*, Palo Alto, CA: Mayfield. (Original work published in 1954.)

Burgoon, J. K., Burgoon, M., & Wilkinson, M. (1981). Writing style as a predictor of newspaper readership, satisfaction and image. *Journalism Quarterly, 58*, 230-231.

Danielson, W. A., & Bryan, S. D. (1964). Readability of wire stories in eight news categories. *Journalism Quarterly, 41*, 105-106.

Flesch, R. (1962). *The art of readable writing.* New York: Collier Books.

Fowler, G. L., Jr. (1978). The comparative readability of newspapers and novels. *Journalism Quarterly, 55*, 589-592.

Fowler, G. L., Jr., & Smith, E. J. (1979). Readability of newspapers and magazines over time. *Newspaper Research Journal, 1*(3), 3.

Fusaro, J. A., & Conover, W. M. (1983). Readability of two tabloid and two non-tabloid newspapers. *Journalism Quarterly, 60*, 142.

Gunning, R. (1952). *The technique of clear writing.* New York: McGraw-Hill.

Hoskins, R. L. (1973). A readability study of AP and UPI wire copy. *Journalism Quarterly, 50*, 360-363.

Larkin, E. F., Grotta, G. L., & Stout, P. (1977, April 8). The 21-34 year old market and the daily newspaper. *ANPA News Research Report No. 1*.

Miller, L. R. (1974). Predictive powers of the Flesch and Bormuth readability formulas. *Journalism Quarterly, 51*, 508-511.

Moznette, J. & Rarick, G. (1968). Which are more readable: Editorials or news stories? *Journalism Quarterly, 45,* 319-324.

Perera, K. (1980). The assessment of linguistic difficulty in reading material. *Educational Review, 32,* 151-161.

Smith, R. F. (1984). How consistently do readability tests measure the difficulty of newswriting? *Newspaper Research Journal, 5*(4), 1.

Stempel, Guido H., III. (1981). Readability of six kinds of content in newspapers. *Newspaper Research Journal, 3*(1), 32.

Newswriting Style

Berner, R. T. (1983). Commentary: The narrative and the headline. *Newspaper Research Journal, 4*(3), 33.

Bogart, L. (1981). *Press and public: Who reads what, where, and why in American newspapers.* Hillsdale, NJ: Lawrence Erlbaum.

Burgoon, J. K., Burgoon, M., & Wilkinson, M. (1981). Writing style as predictor of newspaper readership, satisfaction and image. *Journalism Quarterly, 58,* 230-231.

Cole, R. R., & Shaw, D. L. (1974). "Powerful" verbs and "body language": Does the reader notice? *Journalism Quarterly, 51,* 62-66.

Culbertson, H. M., & Somerick, N. (1976). Cloaked attribution—What does it mean to news readers? *ANPA News Research Bulletin.* American Newspaper Publisher's Association.

Culbertson, H. M., & Somerick, N. (1976). Quotation marks and bylines—What do they mean to readers? *Journalism Quarterly, 53,* 436-467, 508.

Daly, J. A. (1977). The effects of writing apprehension on message encoding. *Journalism Quarterly, 54,* 566-572.

Donohew, L. (1982). Newswriting styles: What arouses the reader? *Newspaper Research Journal, 3*(2), 3.

Donohew, L., Palmgreen, P., & Duncan, J. (1980). An activation model of information exposure. *Communication Monographs,* 295-303.

Grunig, J. E. (1974). Three stopping experiments on the communication of science. *Journalism Quarterly, 51,* 387-399.

Kerrick, J. S. (1959). The inverted pyramid style and attitude change. *Journalism Quarterly, 36,* 487.

Pitts, B. J. (1982). Protocol analysis of the newswriting process. *Newspaper Research Journal, 4*(1), 12.

Shaw, D. L., Protzman, J., & Cole, R. (1982). What do datelines add to a news story? *Journalism Quarterly, 59,* 124-126.

Smith, E. J. (1980). The normative characteristics of the cumulative news story. *Journalism Quarterly, 57,* 292-296, 313.

Smith, R. F., & Voelz, P. (1983). Newspaper stylistic codes: A hindrance to understanding? *Journalism Quarterly, 60,* 641-646, 662.

Stapler, H. (1985). The one-sentence/long-sentence habit of writing leads and how it hurts readership. *Newspaper Research Journal, 7*(1), 17.

Ruffner, M., & Burgoon, M. (1981). The relationship between writing style and personality structure. *Newspaper Research Journal, 2*(2), 28.

Weaver, D. H., Hopkins, W. W., Billings, W. H., & Cole, R. R. (1974). Quotes vs. paraphrases in writing: Does it make a difference to readers? *Journalism Quarterly, 51,* 400-404.

Decision Making by Editors

Atwood, L. E. (1970). How newsmen and readers perceive each others' story preferences. *Journalism Quarterly, 47,* 296-302.

Breed, W. (1955). Newspaper "opinion leaders" and processes of standardization. *Journalism Quarterly, 32,* 277-284, 328.

Breed, W. (1955). Social control in the newsroom: A functional analysis. *Social Forces, 33,* 326-335.

Bowers, D. R. (1967). Activity by publishers in directing newsroom decisions. *Journalism Quarterly, 44,* 43-52.

Buckalew, J. K. (1969). A Q-analysis of television news editors' decisions. *Journalism Quarterly, 46,* 135-137.

Clyde, R. W. (1969). Inter-media standardization: A Q-analysis of news editors. *Journalism Quarterly, 46,* 349-351.

Donohew, L. (1967). Newspaper gatekeepers and forces in the news channel. *Public Opinion Quarterly, 31,* 61-68.

Edelstein, A. S. (1966). *Perspectives in mass communication.* Copenhagen: Einar Harcks Forlag.

Gieber, W. (1956). Across the desk: A study of 16 telegraph editors. *Journalism Quarterly, 33,* 423-442.

Gieber, W. (1960). How "gatekeepers" view local civil liberties news. *Journalism Quarterly, 37,* 199-205.

Lindeborg, R., & Stone, G. (1974). News values as reflected in newspaper content found stable from 1950 through 1970. *Research for Better Newspapers, 7,* 41.

Lippmann, W. (1966). The nature of news. In C. Steinberg (Ed.), *Mass media and communication* (pp. 142-151). New York: Hastings House.

McCombs, M. E., & Shaw, D. L. (1972). The agenda-setting function of mass media. *Public Opinion Quarterly, 36,* 176-187.

Olien, C. N., Donohue, G. A., & Tichenor, P. J. (1968). The community editor's power and the reporting of conflict. *Journalism Quarterly, 45,* 243-252.

Sasser, E. L., & Russell, J. T. (1972). The fallacy of news judgment. *Journalism Quarterly, 49,* 280-284.

Shaw, D. L. (1969). Surveillance vs. constraint: Press coverage of a social issue. *Journalism Quarterly, 46,* 707-712.

Singletary, M. W. (1977, August 12). What determines the news? *ANPA News Research Report No. 5.*

Tuchman, G. (1978). *Making news: A study in the construction of reality.* New York: Free Press.

Ward, W. J. (1967). News values, news situations, and news selections: An intensive study of ten city editors. *Dissertation Abstracts International, 28,* 616-A.

White, D. M. (1950). The "Gatekeeper": A case study in the selection of news. *Journalism Quarterly, 27,* 282-290.

Electronic Editing

Bennett, R., Murray, R. L., & Stampel, G. H., III. (1977, July). "Editing Accuracy Drops with VDTs, Ohio Study Shows." *Journalism Educator, 32,* 11-12.

Crook, J. A. (1977, January). How the new technology affects student editing. *Journalism Educator, 31,* 12-15, 46.

Doebler, P. D. (1974, April). Advantages of electronic editing systems. *Newspaper Production,* p. 6.

Endres, F. F. (1985). Daily newspaper utilization of computer data bases. *Newspaper Research Journal, 7*(1), 29.

Fisher, R. M. (1978, March 27). Editing by pencil found slightly faster than by VDT. *Publisher's Auxilary,* p. 2.

Garrison, B. (1980). The electronic gatekeeper: Editing on the copy desk of a metropolitan newspaper. *Newspaper Research Journal, 1*(3), 7.

Garrison, B. (1982). Electronic editing systems and their impact on news decision making. *Newspaper Research Journal, 3*(2), 43.

Kurtz, L. D. (1980). The electronic editor. *Journal of Communication, 30,* 54-57.

Lindley, W. R. (1977). Does the VDT affect news content? *Journalism Resource Information* (Idaho State University), pp. 2-4.

McDonald, L. (1984, Summer). Commerical database survey. *Bulletin of the Newspaper Division of the Special Libraries Association,* p. 14.

Miller, T. (1983, September). Information, please, and fast: Reporting's revolution: Data bases. *Washington Journalism Review,* pp. 51-53.

Randall, S. D. (1979). Effect of electronic editing on error rate of newspapers. *Journalism Quarterly, 56,* 161-165.

Ruth, M. (1985, July). Electronic library systems reach watershed year. *Presstime,* pp. 10-11.

Shipley, L. J., Gentry, J. K., & Clarke, J. W. (1979). VDT vs. pencil: A comparison of speed and accuracy. University of Missouri monograph. Columbia: University of Missouri School of Journalism.

Sneed, D. (1985). VDTs as potential health hazards: A critical analysis. *Newspaper Research Journal, 6*(4), 66.

Stulce, R. B. (1976). *The effect of electronic writing and editing equipment on the news copy of a newspaper: A content analysis of selected front pages of the Knoxville News-Sentinel.* Unpublished master's thesis, University of Tennessee.

Ullmann, J. (1983). "Tapping the Electronic Library," *The IRE Journal.*

Ward, J., & Hansen, K. A. (1986). Commentary: Information age methods in a new reporting model. *Newspaper Research Journal, 7*(3).

Wolton, D. (1979, July/August). Do you love your VDT? *Columbia Journalism Review,* pp. 37-39.

What to Drop and What to Keep

Mauro, J. B., & Weaver, D. H. (1977, July 22). Patterns of newspaper readership. *ANPA News Research Report No. 4.*

McCombs, M. E. (1977, July 22). What to drop and what to keep? *ANPA News Research Report No. 4.*

Meyer, P. (1978). Models for editorial decision making: The benefits of semi-formality. *Journalism Quarterly, 55,* 77-83.

Meyer, P. (1979, November 21). The comic strip problem. *ANPA News Research Report No. 24.*

Meyer, P. (1985). *The newspaper survival book: An editor's guide to marketing research,* (pp. 76-77). Bloomington: Indiana State University Press.

Subber, R. C., & Schweitzer, J. C. (1980). What to drop and what to keep: A do-it-yourself approach. *Newspaper Research Journal, 1*(4), 38.

The Newshole and Its Content

Bogart, L. (1981). *Press and public.* (Hillsdale, NJ: Lawrence Erlbaum.

Drew, D., & Wilhoit, G. C. (1976). Newshole allocation policies of American daily newspapers. *Journalism Quarterly, 55*, 434-440, 482.

Lindeborg, R. A., & Stone, G. C. (1974). News values as reflected in news content found stable from 1950 to 1970. *ANPA News Research Bulletin, 7*, 3.

Newspaper Advertising Bureau. (1978). *Two dimensions of news: Interest and importance ratings of the editorial content of the American press* (pp. 17-18). New York: Author.

Stone, G. C. (1975). *Management of resources in community-sized newspapers.* Unpublished doctoral dissertation, Syracuse University.

Graphic Design and Packaging

Bain, C., & Weaver, D. (1979). Readers' reactions to newspaper design. *Newspaper Research Journal, 1*(1), 48.

Baxter, W. S., Quarles, R., & Kosak, H. (1978). The effects of photographs and their size on reading and recall of news stories. *ERIC Document Reproduction Service No. 159, 722.*

Click, J. W., & Stempel, G. H., III. (1968). Reader response to newspaper front-page format. *Journal of Typographic Research, 2*, 27-42.

Click, J. W., & Stempel, G. H., III. (1982, July 29). Reader response to front pages with modular format and color. *ANPA News Research Report No. 35.*

Click, J. W., & Stempel, G. H., III. (1979, September 28). Rate of adoption of modern format by daily newspapers. *ANPA News Research Report No. 22, p. 6.*

Garcia, M., Click, J. W., & Stempel, G. H., III. (1981). Reader response to redesign of St. Cloud *Daily Times. Newspaper Research Journal, 2*(2), 36.

Geraci, P. C. (1983). Comparison of graphic design and illustration use in three Washington, D.C., newspapers. *Newspaper Research Journal, 5*(2), 29.

Rarick, G. (1967). *Field experiments in newspaper item readership.* Unpublished manuscript, University of Oregon, Division of Communication Research, Eugene.

Schweitzer, J. C. (1980). Newspaper front pages revisited: Reader reactions. *Newspaper Research Journal, 2*(1), 12.

Schweitzer, J. C., Weaver, D. H., & Stone, G. C. (1977). Morning-evening newspaper circulation: What effect do appearance and content have? *Journalism Quarterly, 54*, 515-522.

Stone, G. C., Schweitzer, J. C., & Weaver, D. H. (1978). Adoption of modern newspaper design. *Journalism Quarterly, 55*, 761-765.

Utt, S. H., & Pasternack, S. (1985). Use of graphic devices in a competitive situation: A case study of 10 cities. *Newspaper Research Journal, 7*(1), 7.

Weaver, D. H., Mullins, L. E., & McCombs, M. E. (1974, December 31). Competing daily newspapers: A comparison of content and format. *ANPA News Research Bulletin No. 8, p. 15.*

Weaver, D. H., Schweitzer, J. C., & Stone, G. C. (1977, April 12). Content, appearance, and circulation: An analysis of individual newspaper characteristics. *ANPA News Research Report No. 12.*

Wolf, R., & Grotta, G. L. (1985). Images: A question of readership. *Newspaper Research Journal, 6*(2), 30.

4

NEWSROOM PERSONNEL AND MANAGEMENT

Learning about news personnel and newsroom management is one of the most recent areas for newspaper research concern, yet one of the most important for the internal health of the industry.

In the early 1980s, the newspaper industry became America's largest production enterprise and its largest private employer. Since such records are not set overnight, we may assume newspapering has always been a labor-intensive business. What is difficult to understand, then, is why there has been so little research on newspaper management.

There may be a number of plausible explanations: (1) press associations and similar organizations provided necessary newspaper-management information at meetings; (2) newspapers were believed to be so distinct an enterprise that no general rules of management could be applied to them; (3) extensive management research was done by the industry on a proprietary basis and has never been available publicly; (4) newspaper researchers were either incapable of doing management research; or (5) researchers were not interested in newspaper management. Many books dating back even to the 1920s were written on how to run a newspaper. But from the mid-1950s to the early 1980s, one text (Rucker and Williams, 1955) dominated the field, and that text was devoted primarily to small newspaper operations.

It's hard to imagine those who became newspaper executives—either through family ties or by rising through the journalistic ranks—had much business training, although they must have possessed considerable business acumen. So it's difficult to explain why research on newspaper management was so scant prior to 1970. In spite of the dearth of management studies, the newspaper industry has thrived over time. In fact, its profitability far out-performed that of American business generally. So, whether the skills existed previously or whether they are only being developed now, there is today both an appreciation of and an interest in newspaper management.

Actually, only since the 1980s has there been any move toward serious study (Sohn, 1981, 1984; discussed below) of newspaper management practices. Yet a body of studies now exists to support some basic precepts. These studies can be grouped into findings on demographics of newspeople; salaries, women, and minorities; hiring, training, and continuing education; motivational needs; and management style. A final, controversial area to be assessed here is the evidence on the merit of group versus independent ownership of papers.

DEMOGRAPHICS OF NEWSROOM PERSONNEL

Recent research has focused on the background and even the philosophy of newspaper personnel, from publishers to reporters. The hypothesis of these studies has been that the executives, editors, and writers are significantly different from the audience who read newspapers. Much of the research has been controversial. Questions have been raised about the intent of researchers who have reported media practitioners are more liberal and generally more elitist than the population and have concluded the media are biased toward liberal positions.

> Depending on which media and which practitioners have been studied, the research shows news people at the larger and more prestigious media institutions are more liberal and higher in socio-economic status than the population generally. However, studies of smaller and less elite institutions show these media practitioners are not vastly different from their audience members.

Gans (1985) offered a critique of recent studies of media practitioners. He concluded the liberal bias Lichter and colleagues (1981, 1982) alleged was not a true picture of journalists' demographics nationally and provided no factual basis for suggesting media presentations are biased toward either a liberal or a conservative position. The most telling analysis comes from Johnstone, Slawski, and Bowman (1976) who reported a significant distinction between the background of journalists at prominent media organizations and those at nonprominent organizations. While those at the elite media were definitely better educated and likely to consider themselves liberal, the demographics and political leanings of nonprominent media journalists were only slightly different from the population generally. Johnstone and other researchers have noted journalists' backgrounds and philosophies are similar to those of people in other professional status positions (see Epstein, 1973; Gans, 1979; Sigal, 1973; Tuchman, 1978). And Gans stated that finding distinct demographic or philosophical differences would not substantiate an accusation that the content of media is being influenced.

These same conclusions were reached by Weaver and Wilhoit (1986) in their 1983 survey of a random sample of 1,001 journalists. In prominent media organizations, 33% of the executives were Democrats, 9% were Republican, and 58% were independents. These figures indicated an increase in independents and an equal decrease in Democrats since 1971. Staffers at the prominent media were 51% Democrat, 4% Republican, and 44% independent; and these figures represented an 8% increase for Democrats, a 12% decrease for Republicans, and a 10% increase for independents since 1971. On nonprominent media, executives and staffers were highly similar in political identification at about 39% Democrat, 21% Republican, and 38% independent. There had been an approximate 5% gain for Democrats, a 9% loss for Republicans, and a 7% gain for independents since 1971. The authors concluded, "U.S. journalists as a whole do not appear to be the 'new liberals' that Lichter and Rothman term their sample of elite journalists." In fact, compared with the U.S. adult population, the left-leaning percentage of journalists is not out of tune with political identifications nationally.

Overall, according to Weaver and Wilhoit, about three-fourths of all daily newspaper journalists and 70% of weekly newspaper journalists are college graduates. The larger the media organization in terms of editorial staff size, the more likely journalists will have a college degree. The researchers noted figures from the annual Dow Jones Newspaper Fund/Gallup survey of journalism and communication graduates showing 53% of them went into media jobs in 1982. The 1983 Weaver and Wilhoit survey figures showed 55% of all working journalists with college degrees had majored in journalism or communications. There was a distinct trend toward more hiring of journalism majors as more than 60% of journalists under age 34 had journalism or communication degrees compared with only 42% of those aged 35 and older.

Schwed's study of daily newspapers (1981) showed there has been an overwhelming trend toward hiring journalism graduates. He reported figures from the Newspaper Fund study of 1970 showing 60% of entry-level posts went to journalism graduates while the comparable 1980 figure was 83%. The majority who were hired from college had previous internships with the paper that hired them. But Schwed noted that half the newsroom hires were from other newspapers while only 28% of hires were directly out of college. Looking at 11 key news executive positions, Schwed found that between 67% and 86% of such executives were college journalism majors, with English majors being the next most prominent educational field. Of the executives, 61% had been originally hired from other newspapers or wire services, but only 7% appointed to the key posts had come from outside their present newspaper: The vast majority of executives had been promoted from within. The city editor post had the most turnover, and this slot was filled by hires from another newspaper about 12% of the time.

Weaver and Wilhoit (1986) provide many other demographic statistics about the journalistic work force. For instance, they report the gross size of the work force increased from 69,500 in 1971 to about 112,000 (a 61% increase) in 1983. The daily newspaper work force went from 38,800 to 51,650, but this represented a 10% drop in daily newspapers' proportion of all working journalists. Weekly newspapers went from 11,500 to 22,942 journalists, a 4% increase in total journalistic work force representation. Younger journalists, those under age 35, constitute 57% of all working journalists, a 12% increase in younger journalists since 1971. The religious background of journalists matches the population exactly with the exception that there are 5.8% Jewish-heritage journalists and only 2% Jewish representation in the population.

SALARIES, WOMEN, AND MINORITIES

A very recent study (Wilson, 1986) offers some key findings about newspaper salaries that apparently apply over time.

Bigger is better. At each position level, those who work for larger newspapers earn more.

Wilson's study, based on a 40% response rate from all 1,600 U.S. daily newspapers, showed that newspaper size determines salaries paid, and size is more influential than position or years of experience. Those who work for newspapers of 100,000-plus circulation earn more than those who are at 50,000-circulation papers, and these journalists earn more than those at 25,000-circulation papers. But it's also true that a more responsible position on any paper pays more than a less responsible position.

Newspaper pay scales are low compared with most other professions. In fact, salaries in journalism, with the exception of television "stars" or large-circulation newspaper publishers or top editors, are usually very low indeed.

Some figures for 1985 presented in the study—given in medians, the point at which half the people at that position earn less and half earn more—were publisher, $55,000; general manager, $45,000; controller, $38,100; editorial page editor, $31,720; advertising director or retail manager, $30,000; top editor, $29,000; business manager or production manager, about $28,600; managing editor, $27,000; longest term copy editor, $22,260; longest term copy desk chief or news editor, $22,000; and longest term reporters, about $16,750. The salaries are generally lower than wages for comparable positions in commerical television and higher than wages in commercial radio.

While salaries for the majority of newsroom personnel are indeed low, two mitigating factors should be remembered. One is that the average size of dailies in the U.S. is about 25,000 circulation and the median circulation level is between 20,000 and 25,000. So, while there are far more newsroom personnel on the staffs of larger papers, there are far more smaller papers in the newspaper industry. Wilson's figures show in fact that the larger dailies pay their longest term reporters about $32,000 while those with circulations under 50,000 are paid from $13,000 to $21,600, in direct proportion to the paper's circulation level. The second mitigating factor is living costs. Although these figures are not presented, other studies show clearly that salary is related to city size as well as circulation size because larger papers are bound to be in larger cities. While a $15,000 annual salary may be unacceptably low for living costs in Dallas, it may be well within the standard family income range in Denton.

The Weaver and Wilhoit (1986) survey reported 1982 median annual income of wire service journalists at $24,100, daily newspaper journalists earned $21,000, and those in weekly newspaper work earned $14,000. The researchers noted that 1982 salaries of all journalists were far below those of comparable occupations, whereas journalists' salaries in 1971 had been closer to those of peers in other fields.

Women in newspaper management have received extensive research recently, due primarily to their near-proportional representation in newsrooms and due to the increase in women media researchers.

Figures from the Johnstone, Slawski, and Bowman (1976) study of American journalists showed women working for prominent media constituted 9% of all executive positions and 22% of staff positions; on nonprominent media the figures were 14% and 27%, respectively. The Weaver and Wilhoit survey of 1983 showed 34% women journalists at daily newspapers and 42% women journalists on weeklies. That was a 12% increase for women at dailies and a 15% increase at weeklies since 1971. The women journalists (all media) earned a median annual wage of just at $15,000; men earned $21,000. However, the salary gaps between sexes were narrow for younger journalists, particularly those under age 25, but were very wide for those older than 35. Still, the figures did suggest equity in salaries for the sexes was taking place with the more recent hires.

Ogan and Weaver (1979) reported there was only one woman manager per U.S. daily paper, regardless of newspaper size, or about 2.4% of newspaper managers were women. These managers were likely to be younger than their male counterparts, unmarried, without children, to be Democrats, and to have parents who were also in managerial occupations. Male and female managers said they worked the same number of hours per week, and the two were equally likely to own company stock. There were few differences between women and men managers in relation to their jobs; however, women managers were more likely to supervise other women and were more likely to say they would hire a woman as their replacement if they left. Ogan and Weaver reported that women were as satisfied with their jobs as were male managers despite being paid significantly less. The women managers at papers with circulations under 50,000 made about $7,000 less than their male counterparts, and those at larger papers made about half what their male peers earned in a year ($17,600 versus $33,500).

At weekly newspapers, one-third of the management-level employees were women, but women constituted the majority of newspaper employees overall. Male managers reported working more hours than their female counterparts and were twice as likely as women to own part or all of the newspaper. Among significant job differences reported, men were twice as likely to make final hiring or promotion decisions, although women were much more likely to make recommendations to superiors. Women were more likely to work part-time, and women were paid less than male managers regardless of their full-time or part-time status.

Based on this study's results, the researchers forecast little improvement in the proportion of women managers at newspapers in the near future.

> Women newspaper managers are greatly under represented in proportion to the number of women in newsrooms. Where they are managers, they are more likely to be low- or mid-level managers rather than top-level. Women also earn significantly less for doing jobs comparable to male managers, and the women are less likely to have families. Yet women managers are equally satisfied with their jobs, although they have less managerial power. There is some evidence of growing equality for women in newspaper management, but the gap is still very wide.

In another study of women newspaper managers, Ogan (1980) found that the educational level and previous job-related experience of women was equal to that of men. However, women managers were much less likely to be currently married or to have children. Male managers supervised more personnel than did female managers, were more likely to have secretarial assistance, spent more time actually managing, and had more budgetary control. While women managers were more likely to receive bonuses, women were paid much less than male managers, as much as $10,000 less. Yet only 35% of the women managers said they were paid less than males doing comparable work at their newspaper, and both sexes said they were satisfied with the pay they received. Asked if they would move to a new location for either a substantial salary increase or a promotion, about 45% of male and female managers said they would not.

Following analysis of this study's data, the researchers reported some optimism about women managers' more equal treatment and the prospects for increase in their representation in newsroom leadership positions.

Jurney (1980) found 212 women held directing editor positions on U.S. daily and Sunday newspapers, or 6.5% of such key posts available. This finding was somewhat higher than had been reported previously, but that may have been an effect of the inclusion of Sunday papers. Sohn (1981) surveyed women newspaper managers in the Rocky Mountain states, including weekly and daily paper managers, and found 17% were women. She identified executive managers among her respondents and reported an annual salary of $16,475 for women and $29,234 for men in the executive group. Male executives were more likely than females to be general managers or business managers, more likely to administer budgets, and more likely to rate themselves as top-level managers. Male executives had more years in the newspaper business but didn't have significantly longer tenure at their present newspaper. In this study male executives were twice as likely as women to say they would accept a move for a substantial salary increase or promotion. Males were more likely to have children, and three times as many women executives as males were divorced or separated. The study showed there were differences in how the male and female executives rated the importance of certain management skills. Women gave highest ratings to not causing trouble, friendships and connections with superiors, ability to handle stress, and technical skills. Men gave more favorable ratings to managerial ability and the ability to think in terms of what's good for the company instead of just oneself.

Ogan (1983) replicated her earlier study in 1982 and found the percentage of women managers at U.S. dailies was 4.5%. This study focused on top-level managers. Men and women managers worked the same 47 hours weekly and both reported high satisfaction with their jobs. Since male managers worked for larger newspapers they had more subordinates, and males reported spending more time in managerial tasks. While more than two-thirds of both sexes had always worked in the newspaper business, women had been at their present newspaper fewer years; yet 45% of the women managers had always worked at their present newspaper versus 28% of the men. Male managers had also held more previous positions than females. About 60% of both sexes said they would accept an offer for promotion at another location. Salary differences remained significant in this study of top-level managers. Males earned an average of $45,500, females an average of $27,300. Men got between $2,000 and $3,000 in bonus, while women got $2,000 or less. The research showed that in 1977 women managers earned 53% of what their male counterparts earned, and in 1983 they earned 60%. Although the percentage had closed in five years, the actual dollar-amount difference had increased. The personal and family characteristics of women managers had not changed during the five-year period.

Sohn (1984) studied newspaper women who were identified by their newspapers as being likely candidates for future top-level management positions and who reported they were interested in becoming top managers. At 33, their average age was below that reported in other studies of women managers, and at $20,424, their average salary was higher than other low- and mid-level women newspaper managers. Sohn found these women managers had: (1) consciously eliminated family and social obligations that might compromise their career goals, (2) set goals that allowed them to state a specific job they wanted to hold in five years, (3) set goals in terms of individual achievement rather than in terms of organizational improvement, and (4) set relatively low career goals for themselves by naming a job only two rungs above their present position as the job they expected to have in five years. Sohn concluded that while these women managers had high commitment, their company orientation and personal aspirations were not as well focused as these managerial indices might have been. But she noted that 70% of them had not yet attended a management-training program at the time they were surveyed.

Perhaps the antithesis of reasons for the recent rash of studies on women in newspapers explains the dearth of studies on minorities:

> Minorities continue not to be represented in the newsroom at—or even near—their proportion in the population.

At this writing, their number in journalism research remains relatively low as well, although it too is improving.

Trayes (1969) documented the percentage of blacks employed in newsrooms of the nation's 20 largest newspaper cities was only 2.8%. Davis and Westmoreland (1974) reported on a 1971 survey of minority editorial representation at 44 Texas daily newspapers. Including all nonwhites, 66 minority persons, or about .5% of total newsroom employees, were tallied. Additionally, more than one-third of the Texas newsroom minorities had been employed within two years of the study, and none was in a management position. Although the sample was quite small, the minority newsroom employee's background and journalistic experience was more diverse than that reported for whites in similar research. Still, neither the minority employees themselves nor their editors noted problems about acceptance in the newsroom or by news sources.

In a 10-year follow-up to his original study (Trayes, 1979) found the number of blacks in major metropolitan newsrooms had nearly doubled. The American Society of Newspaper Editors (1984) study of newsroom staff found only 5.8% minorities and lamented that the slow increase in minority representation existed in spite of a commitment by U.S. newspapers to meet a goal of proportional minority representation by the year 2000.

Guimary (1984) studied all minority representation in newsrooms of six California metropolitan papers and reported higher proportional representation than previous studies: The proportion of minorities was 9.4% in 1979 and 12.7% in 1984. While these figures are certainly higher than those reported nationally, they represent only those newspapers that participated in the study. Furthermore, at the time the study was conducted California's minority population was 22%, while the national proportion was 17% minority. Finally, the Guimary study included the Oakland *Tribune,* in a city with a 67% minority, which has just 20% minority staffers.

The Weaver and Wilhoit survey showed the percentage of minorities in journalism (all media) was lower than other recent estimates. Blacks represented 2.9% of the population; Hispanics, .6%, and Asians, .4%.

HIRING, TRAINING, AND CONTINUING EDUCATION

Some of the material that might belong here has been presented in the previous sections on demographics and on salaries, women, and minorities. For instance, the Schwed (1981; demographics) study reported newspapers get most staffers from other papers and about three-fourths of all newsroom personnel are journalism graduates. There are, however, a number of research insights about hiring, training, and continuing education that help present a more complete picture of how newspapers select and nurture their newsroom employees.

Trayes (1976) surveyed 52 executives at Associated Press Managing Editors' (APME) newspapers. He found editors on 45 dailies were instrumental in screening and hiring personnel for their newsrooms. Only about one-fourth of the editors said they were actively recruiting in 1974, and these were seeking interns from campuses, minorities and women. The editors provided the following attributes they sought of new hires:

Personal Characteristics: (a) personality and character; (b) nature of the person's ambitions; (c) appearance and grooming; and (d) personal habits. Experience: (a) experience on other dailies; (b) journalism education; and (c) campus paper experience. Backing: (a) references; and (b) who recommended. Traits: (a) comprehension; (b) language craftsmanship; (c) awareness and curiosity; (d) growth potential; (e) judgment; (f) cooperativeness; and (g) spelling ability.

Trayes reported only half the APME dailies usually test newsroom employees before hiring them. Most of the tests used were written and covered these elements of the profession: spelling; story organization and writing; language, grammar, and word definitions; general knowledge; typing, copyediting; special field capability; and practice source interview. The tests were usually developed by the newspapers themselves, but they were not decisive in hiring decisions. Only 7 of 38 newspapers responding to the survey gave newsroom applicants psychological tests.

Most of the editors also were instrumental in the decision to promote or reassign newsroom employees. Almost none used any kind of test to help make these decisions; and editors explained they got necessary information in other ways, they had no examples of such tests, or they didn't think tests would be effective. Trayes was highly critical of newspaper's lack of sophistication in hiring and promoting newsroom employees. He strongly recommended use of tests, noted editors should solicit input from other newsroom managers (which they did infrequently), and advocated job openings be advertised. Trayes said the personal characteristics used in hiring were laudable—sex, marital status, and race were not considered—but such characteristics were extremely difficult to measure, particularly without psychological tests.

Evidence indicates newspaper hiring practices are becoming more sophisticated. Skills testing is more extensive and is used more frequently, and the industry has developed an on-the-job tryout.

More recently, Smith (1982) studied screening techniques used in hiring by a small national sample of newspapers with circulations under 120,000. He found 34% of the newspapers used written tests, another 34% used written tests and short-term tryouts, and 5% used the tryouts but no test. A total of 24% of the papers used neither screening procedure. Newspaper size had no bearing on whether screening was used.

Most of the papers had devised their own tests and the tests varied greatly. Some were very short and others took up to three hours. Spelling was the single most tested skill and words were either commonly misspelled words or words journalists encounter frequently. More than 90% of the tests included grammar and word usage sections, and an equally high percentage of tests included writing and editing sections. Editing job candidates often got an additional test of their editing skills. Short-term tryouts were defined as a one- or two-week apprenticeship during which the candidate handled day-to-day activities and after which the candidate might or might not be hired by the newspaper. Short-term tryouts are different from the 90-day or six-month probationary period most newspapers require. The tryouts were three to five days on 41% of papers that used them; one-day tryouts were used by 27%; one-week tryouts were used by 20%; and only 12% used tryouts between one and two weeks. Tryout applicants received salaries in 87% of the cases, and the rates were either beginning reporter or union scale. Most editors said they tried three to five applicants before deciding whom to hire.

Unions, while not a real force in the newsroom, have influenced newspaper policies and practices from their positions of strength in production departments. Barwis (1981) studied the effect of new technology on newspaper employment. She forecast continuing losses to the ranks of craft unions, reduced bargaining power for individual unions, growing interest in union mergers, greater profitability for publishers, reduced proportion of total newspaper budget devoted to wages, and greater salary differential between editorial and production workers. In all, she predicted automation in newspaper production would continue to hurt the craft unions and might increasingly benefit editorial employees.

In an earlier study, Barwis (1978) looked at inroads made by the Newspaper Guild in gaining reporter power or newsroom democracy.

While it represented nearly 40% of daily newspaper and wire service reporters in the mid-1970s, the union was depicted as being more successful in representing employees in economic matters rather than securing employee participation in newsroom-management decisions. Newsroom democracy is linked with the liberal movement of the late 1960s since the union adopted its reporter power position in 1970. However, industrial communications researchers have long recognized employee participation in decision making can improve worker attitude, interest, and effectiveness. But Barwis's research showed only 2 of 18 possible democracy provisions the union advocated had been written into a majority of contracts: (1) An employee's byline could not be used over his or her protest and (2) the guild could designate a member committee to negotiate with management on matters arising from the application of the contract affecting employee and employer relations. Although the latter item opened the door to extensive reporter participation in newsroom policy—and real reporter power might have begun at some papers—the study found the guild had not gotten far with the movement. In fact, a majority of those contracts containing voice, integrity, and privilege provisions had first been signed prior to 1945 when the guild had been in existence only 12 years.

Fedler and Taylor (1981) reported findings from a national sample of newspaper reporters in an investigation of the Newspaper Guild's influence on journalists' salaries and the likelihood of journalists joining a union. Providing statistics from other studies, Fedler and Taylor noted U.S. union growth had declined steadily since 1945 but white-collar unions had experienced dramatic gains. Still, only 45% of all journalists belonged to a professional organization, and only about 13% of newspeople belonged to a national professional organization. Less than 25% of the nation's dailies have any unions.

> Unions are more likely to be in place at larger papers, but would probably have more effect on increasing salaries at smaller papers since the larger papers already pay higher wages to all newsroom employees.

Findings from the Fedler and Taylor study were: (1) About 38% of the originally listed reporters said they had been promoted; (2) about 30% of respondents had completed some graduate work; (3) more experienced journalists who worked for larger papers and belonged to unions earned the highest wages; (4) 75% of the journalists were satisfied with their jobs, and satisfaction was not related to salary level; and (5) salary level was dependent more on paper size than on any other single factor, including whether the journalist belonged to a union.

Journalists are not philosophically opposed to unions. While older, more experienced reporters have the opportunity to join unions, only half do. Younger, less experienced reporters say they would join unions if they were available at their papers, but few journalists are interested in organizing unions at their papers either through fear of retribution or because they are content with their present situation.

The research had hypothesized reporters who were very interested in improving the media's professional standards would be less likely to join unions, but this was unsupported. Instead, younger reporters were more interested in improving standards regardless of education or union membership. Some 33% of the respondents did belong to a union, and they were the older, more experienced reporters who worked for larger newspapers. At the same time that younger reporters indicated they would have joined a union had one been available, older, more experienced reporters had more opportunity to join a union but half had not joined. Those who had declined union membership said working conditions and wages and their papers were already fair. Reporters who thought their bosses opposed a union were less likely to have joined; those with the lowest salaries were most likely to believe they needed a union. Half the reporters who did not have a union available said they would join one if it were available, and the inclination to join was directly related to current job satisfaction and to being younger. Fear of some form of retaliation by newsroom bosses was the chief reason reporters said they wouldn't try to organize a union.

This chapter's early speculation about management practices of newspapers suggested much personnel training might be provided through continuing education workshops and seminars. A number of such employee improvement projects are known to be offered by the major newspaper groups, by media foundations, and by corporations with an interest in improving coverage of their businesses. In addition, newspapers frequently send selected newsroom personnel to university courses in a variety of disciplines or invite professors to the newsroom for a variety of activities including giving staffers lessons in precision journalism or serving as writing coaches (Pease 1986). Not much research has been devoted specifically to continuing education practices, but there are some hints of the extent to which newspapers are involved in such training procedures.

Ogan (1983) found 90% of men and 83% of women managers had participated in some form of management training, primarily seminars. An additional 24% of the women managers reported attending both in-house and off-site training experiences. Her respondents also said they had attended courses at a university. The training was paid for by the newspaper in 78% of the instances mentioned by male managers and in 87% of the instances women managers mentioned. Male managers belonged to an average of 1.6 professional organizations; women managers belonged to an average 1.7. Sohn and Chusmir (1985) found 74% of executive males had been given an opportunity to participate in management-training programs versus only 54% of women executives. Of those who did attend, nearly 95% of the women and 86% of the men said they would attend another training seminar if it were available. For both sexes of executive managers, "The most common situation is for the newspaper to have paid for any training received." Ogan (1980) reported the employer paid total costs of management-training seminars in 88% of the cases for both sexes. Such training consisted of in-house and off-site seminars and courses taken at local universities. In this sample, 67% of the men and 52% of the women had participated in a mangement seminar, and an additional 28% of men and 11% of women had been involved in a second type of training program. The researcher said attending management-training programs typically required being nominated by the employer, and responding executives considered selection a sign of promotability. Of those who had not participated in such training, 32% of the men and 42% of the women said no one had asked them to attend. Ogan and Weaver (1979) found few of their daily newspaper women managers belonged to any media-related women's organizations. Of the newspapers in the sample that offered a management-training program, 80% of the program's current participants were male. This last finding was considered a pessimistic forecast for the future of women managers.

Several studies have attempted to apply general employee tests to newsroom personnel. Some types of evaluations used by other businesses have been successfully applied to newspapers; some have not. For instance Joseph (1983) applied the Michigan Alcoholism Screening Test to newsroom personnel at 14 randomly selected U.S. newspapers. The test is a standard method for measuring alcoholism, and such tests have documented an average of 10% alcoholic rate among all adults who drink. Joseph found editors had a 21% rate of alcoholism, and reporters had a 23% rate. Male editors' rate of alcoholism was 26%; female editors' was 10%. But among reporters, males had a 26% rate of alcoholism and females a 20% rate. While the researcher cautioned against drawing cause-and-effect implications from the study, he emphasized the female reporter rate of alcoholism is twice the national average for females, and the rate of alcoholism in the newsroom overall denotes a serious problem.

While the Joseph inquiry shows a general management tool can be applied beneficially to newsroom problems, other researchers have not had the same success in adapting general business applications to the newsroom situation.

Management principles should offer the best approaches to studying the journalistic workplace, but newspaper researchers only recently have begun employing business theories in newsroom situations.

Johnstone, Slawski, and Bowman's landmark study of newsroom employees (1976) is a case in point. Here sociologists tried to account for journalists' satisfaction with their work. Demographic variables were found less effective than motivational variables in predicting work satisfaction. The methodological conclusion is that management principles could be used effectively by newspaper researchers, but researchers aren't yet familiar enough with these principles. Other studies have also shown that the management tools can't be applied easily to the newsroom workplace, due in part to the uniqueness of the newsroom work environment and journalistic personnel.

Chusmir (1983) looked at three needs all types of workers have: need for achievement, to do something better than before; need for affiliation, the desire for friendship, love, and belonging; and need for power, the need to control the means of influence over others. Chusmir said when a worker's needs match the job's requirements, the worker is likely to have higher interest, satisfaction, and total job commitment—all leading to higher quality performance. He matched journalistic job requirements with the three worker need levels and offered the guidelines for matches in Table 4.1.

Chusmir found many newsroom jobs are associated with a power need. Newspapers recruit college graduates who usually have a high achievement drive, but students don't always possess the power drive associated with success in newsroom jobs. The researcher suggested motivational testing prior to hiring and advised newsroom managers to consider motivational scores "all other things being equal." A more likely application for the thematic apperception tests is using them in promotion and reassessment decisions. The tests might reduce the possibility of placing a newsroom employee in a job he or she is less capable of performing or may be uncomfortable doing. Chusmir noted some jobs at a newspaper have low motivational levels on all three need dimensions. He suggested management seek ways to enrich these jobs through positive reinforcement, quality circles, and so forth.

While the Chusmir study holds great potential as a newsroom

TABLE 4.1
Motivational Needs Associated with Newsroom Jobs

Job Classification	Power	Achievement	Affiliation
Writers whose writing is related to personal experience (critics, editorial writers, columnists)	=	=	=
Departmental editors (city, sports, life-style, bureau, makeup, news, metro, state) and morgue librarians	=	=	=
Newswriters, reporters, wire editors, and rewrite people	+	=	=
Managing and executive editors	+	=	−
Photojournalists, graphic artists and designers, cartoonists	=	+	−
Publisher and general manager	+	=	−

NOTE: + is greater need; = is moderate need; - is less need. (From "Profile of the Motivational Needs of Individuals in the Newspaper Industry" by L. H. Chusmir, 1983, *Newspaper Research Journal, 5.* Copyright 1983 by Newspaper Research Journal. Reprinted by permission.)

screening and management tool, it has not been sufficiently tested. Before making hiring, assignment, or promotion decisions based on motivational scores, the newspaper industry should undertake careful assessment of the tests' validity, possibly through a significant number of individual case studies on newsroom personnel.

Sohn and Chusmir (1985) applied the Chusmir-developed need scales to newspaper managers and owners. They found publishers expressed more of a power need than their entrepreneurial counterparts nationwide, and the newspaper managers sampled expressed less achievement need. Affiliation need was not a factor at all. The researchers suggested journalists at all levels might have a strong need for power, but the power need might be particularly acute for those in management positions. A recommendation was that reward systems for newsroom success—especially to those journalists being groomed for management—should focus on public recognition or should result in greater control over newsroom colleagues. The researchers also found the longer a manager holds a job, the more satisfied he or she will be with the job. Here it was recommended that newsroom managers be given special nurturing in their early years as managers. The researchers failed to find a link between need fit, job satisfaction, and commitment—a finding that has been the case in many similar professions. It was also noted that

57% of the subjects had low job commitment, and 59% of subjects with good job need fits had low job commitment. These findings could not be explained by current knowledge on this aspect of newspaper management.

Another recent study attempted to apply brain hemisphericity to newsroom management considerations. Vannatta (1981) studied left-brain versus right-brain dominance and applied distinctions between the two physiological types. The brain's left hemisphere is the source of logic and analysis, linguistic activity, and thinking language. The right hemisphere is the intuitive portion of thought and is associated with seeing the pattern of things, orientation, abstract thinking, and the appreciation of forms and artistic talents. Using a multiple choice test form (Your Style of Learning and Thinking, Form A), Vannatta classified a sample of 100 newspaper journalists into left-brain dominant or right-brain dominant, or integrative information-processing styles. She found some support for journalists' having both left-brain dominant and integrated cognitive styles; reporters tended to be left-brain dominated, while editors and photographers used integrated styles. Overall, journalists were said to prefer the integrated style. Her findings suggested reporting hard news and business writing was a left-brain procedure; writing research articles, copyediting, general assignment reporting, or being a news manager required an integrated style; and sports, photography, and feature writing were right-brain dominant. She recommended testing job applicants for brain dominance and devising training for those acceptable applicants who had not already developed techniques that would aid them in the job they would be hired to perform. But Vannatta cautioned that more research on the brain hemisphericity of journalists is needed before using the tests to full advantage.

MANAGEMENT-STYLE CONSIDERATIONS

A recent study (Trayes, 1978) provides some insight about how daily newspapers' newsrooms are managed. There is, in fact, a wide variety of possible structures that depend either on size of the paper or individual practices. Managing editors find themselves both managers of people and editors of newspapers. Which of the functions dominates depends on the newspaper size, with those at larger papers serving the management function more. Those at smaller dailies participate more in producing the news-editorial product. These middle managers may report to one or more executives before the command chain reaches the publisher (57% operate this way), or managing editors may report directly to the publisher (31% do). Managing editors may supervise assistant management editors, who then supervise newspaper department editors; or the managing editor may be the direct supervisor of section editors. On some papers, each department operates almost independently, while at others staff personnel are pooled and assigned to specific sections as the need arises.

There is no accepted staffing pattern at daily newspaper newsrooms. Instead, the number of reporters, editors, and executives varies widely.

Trayes, in doing the study, marveled at the vast differences in personnel staffing even of newspapers in the same circulation size category. He said there is wide variance in the numbers of executives and reporters per paper, although the larger papers certainly do have a larger median staff size. Only 10% of the sample sent an official, written job description, and Trayes said managing editors "appear to have virtual 'blank checks' as far as their newsroom roles are concerned." The researcher portrayed managing editors as devoting about one-third of their time to managing and one-third to editing, and almost none did much staff recruiting, arranging in-service training, or meeting or socializing with their staff. Further, managing editors were given little or no management training: They had not served temporarily in a nonnewsroom department, been to management seminars, or had any other form of special preparation for the new administrative positions they were taking.

Given the variety of management structures and the lack of administrative training, how well might newsroom leaders be expected to perform? The research, where there is any evidence, indicates newsroom management styles are comparable to those of other industries.

Effective communication is considered the key to successful management; so newsroom managers' communication patterns are important in any consideration of management styles. Kaufman (1981) looked at differences attributable to bilateral and unilateral newspaper organization. Based on prevailing theories of how management structure might affect organizational communication, Kaufman predicted bilateral administration—designed for extensive interdepartmental communication—would result in a better interaction-influence system for the newspaper. Applying business administration tests to personnel at two newspapers with differing types of organizational structure, Kaufman found the bilateral type actually resulted in a less effective organizational system than the unilateral type. Kaufman suggested both types of organizational structure had the potential to increase interaction-influence. While the bilateral form promoted better relationships at the top executive level, it could result in more dissension among lower-level personnel. He said further research on different samples of newspapers might show the bilateral administration form was superior, but his one-shot study was inconclusive.

Fowler and Shipman (1984) reported findings from a small-sample study of the over-30,000 circulation papers in Pennsylvania. These newsroom managers were found to be highly involved in personal interaction with employees. They evaluated employees regularly (69%), and almost all of them participated personally in newsroom hirings. Communication with employees was done either face-to-face or through newsroom subeditors. Of course personal communication decreased as size of the newspaper increased. Staff meetings occurred on a daily or weekly basis at 90% of these newspapers. While editors thought this form of communication was effective, they said there was room for improvement. Almost all editors said they critiqued their newspaper frequently, but the results of critiques were communicated to employees through their most direct editor. The more frequent were critiques, the less frequent were employee evaluations.

> The ideal newsroom situation is one of open communication where editors talk to employees personally and where employees feel they are free to say what they wish. This employee attitude is related to interest in what editors have to say, the level of belief employees have in information they receive, the comfort level editors feel when they must be absent from the newspaper for extended periods, and employees' feeling of participation.

Recent studies of newsroom management have focused on reporter "participation" in decision making. The controversy was most intense during the early 1970s when reporters sought some control over story selection, editing, and story play. Barwis (1978) studied the progress made by the Newspaper Guild in bargaining with publishers on reporter power or newsroom democracy issues. She found only 2 of 18 bargaining planks were adopted by a majority of guild papers: the existence of a guild bargaining committee to negotiate with management; and not using a byline over a reporter's objection. Further analysis showed these guild successes in newsroom participation actually occurred when the union began in the 1940s rather than as a result of more recent reporter or guild activity. But, while formal changes in newsroom participation have been minimal, the concept—

reporters and editors having a dialogue about what happens with the news process—is considered a good one simply because it opens channels of communication.

In a study of management decisions at a sample of some 350 dailies, Joseph (1981) found reporters were given equal voice in story suggestions, writing and reporting time needed, how to cover a story, and story length. On which stories to cover, reporters either have an equal voice or give input with management making the final decision. Management decision following reporter input is the usual procedure for 17 newsroom policy matters involving the way stories are planned, reported, and edited and in reporter evaluations. Management decides a host of matters related to budgets, salaries and fringes, hiring and firing, promotions, and content placement, without reporter input. The researcher noted reporters at smaller papers are slightly more involved in decision making than are those at larger papers. He speculated that as newspapers increase in size, management becomes more centralized, and centralized management systems are less permissive with employees.

Participation in newsroom decisions was investigated by Joseph (1982a, 1982b) through a national sample of some 500 newspaper managing editors and city-county reporters. On papers of 100,000-plus circulation, reporters and editors disagreed on about half the decision-making practices presented. Reporters wanted equal voice in: byline assignments, how to cover stories, time needed to write and report, story suggestions, overtime needed, which stories to cover, and length of story. Editors wanted input from reporters on these practices but wanted to make the final decisions themselves. Editors' preference was the existing policy on these practices.

Reporters in the Joseph study wanted input to: evaluating and hiring editors, reporters' raises and promotions, editorial budgets, disciplining reporters, determining story page, editorial page direction, promoting management, and selecting columnists. Editors wanted management to make these decisions with little or no reporter input. Again, the editors' preference was existing policy.

While the existing policy did not allow as much reporter input as both reporters and editors believed was needed, reporters and editors agreed reporters should be involved in decisions about: killing a story, final editing, newsroom plans, beat assignment and transfers, and reporter training.

On papers with from 50,001 to 100,000 circulation, the reporter-editor agreement was greater. There was general agreement on input for assignments and content, and agreement that reporters should not participate in personnel or salary decisions. Since reporters on these medium-sized newspapers don't seek as much participation as those on the larger papers, existing practices were closer to their ideal. However, reporters at the medium-sized papers do want input (but not equal voice) on salary, fringes, raises and promotions, editorial budgets, story page and columnist selection. Editors wanted no reporter input on these matters, and that was the existing situation. On the smallest papers in the study, again fewer disagreements emerged because reporters didn't seek as much voice.

While Joseph concluded there is more agreement than conflict on newspaper management practices, he cautioned that opposing views in the newsroom can adversely affect employee participation, satisfaction, and commitment to the workplace. Although his research was exploratory, the findings reported earlier about journalists' need for power suggest management might improve the newsroom environment through increased reporter participation in at least some work-related decision making.

> Journalists generally love their work, but there is growing concern that without greater participation in decision making, job dissatisfaction will drive some newspaper journalists from the industry.

Ziter (1981) based a plea for more innovative newsroom management on the quality of work life (QWL) experiment at the Minneapolis-St. Paul papers. He argued a more participatory, human resources approach to newsroom policy decisions would result in greater cooperation and satisfaction among staff members for their daily work. Ziter and Weaver and Wilhoit (1986) raise the issue of increased worker job dissatisfaction. Weaver and Wilhoit noted a 9% decrease in the number of journalists saying they were very satisfied. Burgoon, Burgoon, and Atkin (1982) reported that although journalists complain about their jobs and the related stress, they love their work—a research finding that has been replicated with virtually every study on journalists' job satisfaction. Yet their study found greater job satisfaction expressed by journalists who said they received clear directives from superiors and who reported greater autonomy related to job satisfaction, particularly among younger journalists. Those journalists aged 40 and younger based job satisfaction on: their esteem for the organization, feedback from superiors, autonomy, and the journalist's own perception of how important salary was to job satisfaction.

Johnstone, Slawski, and Bowman's sample (from 1971) showed only 7% of journalists were dissatisfied and intended to leave the field (primarily the younger reporters who had not yet reached a specialty level); the Weaver-Wilhoit dissatisfaction level had climbed to about 11%, and these potential defectors were more likely to be mid-career journalists with more education and job autonomy. Burgoon, Bernstein, Burgoon, and Atkin (1984) found 16% of a sample of journalists saying they would not remain in journalism "for as long as I can work," and another 16% being neutral on their fidelity to the field. This study found a direct link between journalists' desire to remain in the field and their attitude toward their newspaper, its future, and the public service it performed. Burgoon and associates also linked attitude and job satisfaction with journalists' interpersonal communication habits.

Bennett (1985) studied California editors and noted they felt more comfortable with their journalistic skills than with their management skills. A total of 68% of these editors said they spent at least half their time supervising or managing, and 62% had participated in either on-the-job management training or had attended management-training seminars. More than half of the editors said having the training prior to being appointed a manager would have been very valuable. They rated the out-of-shop management-training programs superior to the in-house training they received, and they believed more attention to management training would help them solve numerous newsroom management problems they faced daily. The editors said the pressures of their jobs were more demanding than those of executives outside the newspaper business and the salary rewards were less. Bennett reported 78% of these editors had been in their current position less than five years and commented the turnover rate for these executives was excessive.

Although research has documented journalists' desire for greater feedback from supervisors, more involvement in decision making and better access to methods of attaining job growth (continuing education, for instance), there is little evidence these roads to job satisfaction are being adequately provided. Mentioned earlier was greater access to management-training seminars, but Weaver and Wilhoit (1986) noted as well that the percentage of journalists who said they would like more continuing education increased from 58% in 1971 to 77% in 1982-1983. Pettus (1981) described a peer review process at Nashville's *The Tennessean* as a method of both increasing feedback and involving the newsroom in critiques of the newspaper product. Flatt (1980) described a Management by Objectives plan at a chain-owned paper that increased newsroom interaction on short- and long-range planning for the editorial staff. There is evidence also in trade publications and newspaper organization newsletters of extensive continuing education programs available to journalists. And a recent, positive sign is the publication of two newspaper management texts: *Newspaper Leadership* (Sohn, Ogan, & Polich, 1986) and *Newsroom Management Handbook* (American Society of Newspaper Editors Foundation, 1985). Similar texts are in press at this time.

This recent interest in newspaper management is certainly a good sign, but it is unclear if these developments will be sufficient to fill the near-void in newspaper management that has existed. Certainly, there has been too little research interest in newspaper management topics.

THE WEIGHT OF CHAINS

One of the continuing themes of newspaper research during the past two decades is an assessment of the effects of media concentration, particularly the growth of newspaper chains or groups. Media observers have been extremely critical of newspaper ownership concentration, and their concern has been with the loss of independent voices. Newspaper researchers have focused on measurable outcomes: the effect of chains on the flow of news, on the market for local media, on newspaper employees, or on newspaper management practices.

Numerous studies have been done since the Commission on Freedom of the Press (1947) first raised the newspaper monopoly issue. The overwhelming outcome of these studies is:

> There is no discernible, adverse effect consistently attributable to newspaper chain ownership.

If the statement appears hedged with qualifiers, it is meant to be. Some studies have found positive or negative effects associated with chains, but in overview, research has failed to make a case that chain ownership, per se, is either a blessing or a threat to the newspaper industry.

Stempel (1973) reported studies in the 1950s and 1960s that showed audience attitude toward newspapers was *more* favorable following a merger. The studies also showed a paper in competition was more likely to engage in sensational news treatment, and a newspaper's merger did not result in reduced news-to-advertising ratios. Stempel (1966) pointed out that 88% of single-owner-newspaper cities had broadcast media that served as competition to the papers.

But in a study of three matched cities, one of which was a total media monopoly and two of which had media competition, Stempel (1973) found residents of the monopoly city were less well informed and used the mass media less. Those in the monopoly city were more likely to be relying on their local paper than an out-of-town paper (although nonlocal media were available to all three cities). Monopoly citizens were as accepting of their mass media as were citizens in the other two towns and nationally. In analyzing news media content in the three cities, Stempel showed that broadcast media in the monopoly town were getting fewer exclusive stories than those in the nonmonopoly towns. He concluded the monopoly media were less competitive and the audience was provided less local news, although the news offered was similar in terms of values and topics presented. The most striking difference was the number of newspaper editorials on local topics in the three cities. While the monopoly city paper ran half as many editorials as the nonmonopoly papers, it ran only four local-issue editorials in a four-week period compared with about 50 run in each of the other two cities. All three papers were equally willing to take stands on issues. Stempel said his findings showed that a total market monopoly was associated with less service to the community. The chief problems with total monopoly were: (1) Broadcast media owned by the local newspaper were less vigorous competitors, and (2) audiences in monopoly towns were more dependent on the local media while being more complacent with its offerings.

Becker, Beam, and Russial (1978) compared measures of newspaper performance with characteristics of the community and the newspaper's organizational structure. They found no significant relationship between newspaper competition and newspaper performance, indicating either monopoly or nonmonopoly papers might be superior performers. Stone, Stone, and Trotter (1981) also reported no relationship between newspaper quality and whether a newspaper belonged to a chain.

Browning, Grierson, and Howard (1984) looked at coverage of Knoxville's International Energy Exposition by a paper that had become chain-owned. The research attempted to determine if the new group ownership would result in less coverage of an issue that had negative implications for local business. This research found no significant change attributable to chain ownership of the newspaper. But Donohue, Olien, and Tichenor (1985) found there was considerable change in conflict reporting among a small sample of Minnesota dailies. Those with in-state ownership contained 50% more column inches of local conflict than out-of-state-ownership papers, and the in-state-owned papers contained three times as much conflict in local government as the out-of-state-owned papers.

Pasadeos (1984) did find some distinct changes in coverage and display resulting from a chain's new purchase. In this case, the San

Antonio *News* went from Harte-Hanks's to Rupert Murdoch's group, becoming Murdoch's first American newspaper. The research showed the *News* became more sensational, both graphically and in the proportion of sensational news stories carried during the first year. The paper also increased the proportion of local news on the front page, so it was less clear if improved offerings of local news or the sensational treatment (or both) accounted for a 14,000 increase in circulation in the first three years Murdoch owned it.

Tillinghast (1984) looked at reporter and source perceptions of bias in the two San Jose, California, dailies after the merger between Knight and Ridder newspapers in 1974. Prior to the merger, the papers were considered biased on almost all of 10 social and institutional issues. Following the merger, bias was seen as significantly diminished "almost to neutral reporting, and in two cases the bias was reversed."

Rarick and Hartman (1966) had reported that with intense competition, newspapers devote more space to local content and that a larger proportion of space would be sensational or human-interest content. Schweitzer and Goldman (1975) looked at the same kinds of questions. Here two local dailies in Bloomington, Indiana, had competed, and then one had gone out of business. The researchers investigated how the remaining paper's content might have changed from the competition to the noncompetition years. Schweitzer and Goldman found no decline in local content following the advent of monopoly and no indication of greater emphasis on sensational news either during intense competition or when the remaining paper was a monopoly. This study also confirmed Stempel's finding:

> The reading audience perceives little difference in newspaper content regardless of whether there is local market newspaper competition.

McGrath and Gaziano (1986) also found people were not well-informed about their daily newspaper's ownership. Audiences didn't know if their paper was chain-owned or independent, but those papers in a competitive situation were rated more credible generally. People who thought their paper was locally owned gave it slightly higher credibility ratings. These findings clearly show audiences don't know if their paper is independent. There is not enough evidence to conclude independent newspapers are believed to be more credible.

When it became clear chain ownership could not be linked with a pattern of adverse effects on the public, attention was turned to possible effects on newspaper economics. Several researchers looked at price effects by chain ownership and concluded if there were such effects, they were minimal. Blankenburg (1983) studied 54 Gannett papers and found it would cost a local merchant between 8% and 18% more for an ad in a Gannett paper than for the same ad in a comparable non-Gannett paper. But Blankenburg attributed the difference to "the background presence of a vigorous, knowledgeable corporation that has the motives and means" to get higher ad rates. Instead of monopoly, the research showed the chain's corporate experience in newspaper economics and marketing could result in individual papers earning a premium advertising rate.

Blankenburg (1982) used the Gannett papers and a non-Gannett matched set to determine if there was a conscious effort by the chain to increase profits by eliminating the least desirable circulation. He found Gannett's circulation had decreased in a 10-year period (ending in 1979) during high newspaper production cost increases. The non-Gannett dailies had increased circulation during the same time period. Blankenburg credited the chain with knowing how to maximize profitability by controlling circulation, another economic benefit of the more sophisticated management attributed to the chain. The researcher acknowledged circulation control was the right eonomic move but suggested the strategy resulted in some residents' being denied a newspaper.

Economic implications of chain ownership have extended beyond cost and management efficiencies attributed to the chain. Some studies have suggested:

> The real influence of chains is their pressure on local publishers to meet profit expectations. With groups, a manager's allegiance is to the central chain. Success means a chance to leave the community for a better position at a larger newspaper.

In a newsroom case study of a 17,000-circulation paper during its merger with a large chain, Soloski (1979) found several changes took place. First, the new group's wire service supplied a torrential flow of news and features that the local paper was urged to use after local and state copy, but before using the AP wire. The local paper came to rely on the group wire and dropped several features it had been purchasing from a syndicate. In addition, the group wire provided copy for special feature sections timed for seasonal events, and the local paper used this service to sell ads around the copy in these sections.

Second, although previously the local paper had been getting editorial columnists' material through the mail and processing it for publication, the paper could now pay for columnists the wire carried and use the wire-fed material without separate processing. However, only those columnists selected by the group's wire were available for the cost savings of not handling columns sent through the mail.

Third, the newspaper's publisher was no longer an independent owner but became part of the group's management team. As such, budget planning done by the publisher had to be approved by corporate headquarters. Further, the publisher was under pressure to meet or exceed the profit goals set. Since the publisher had ambitions to climb the corporate ladder—or at least be promoted to a larger newspaper in the group—he was always conscious of the bottom line. The paper was kept short of newsroom staff, overtime was eliminated, and travel expenses were cut. Each executive on the newspaper received a percentage of the paper's profit as a bonus.

Finally, the group's Management By Objective (MBO) system for the newsroom emphasized the number and readability of reporters' stories, and the wages paid all newspaper employees were set at a rate just high enough to neutralize unionizing efforts.

The picture painted by the study is that of subtle change driven either by employee ambitions of advancing through the group or by financial considerations the group brings to its member papers.

Dertouzos and Thorpe (1982) looked at newspaper groups and determined there were no managerial distinctions that separated them from independents. The chain papers were not found to be superior in using economies of scale, pecuniary economies, or technological diffusion.

Lacy (1985) looked at competition's possible effects on small daily and weekly newspapers in the standard metropolitan statistical areas of city papers. He predicted the smaller papers would be more concerned with monopoly center-city papers than with metropolitan papers in competitive situations. He found the smaller paper publishers in a 20-mile range of the central city thought nonmonopoly papers were an advertising threat and monopoly papers were a circulation threat.

In the economic area, chain ownership can result in grave decisions as well. The sensitivity to profits might force a chain to close a newspaper when the signs indicate it will become an unprofitable burden to the organization. Blankenburg (1985) found that circulation size, trends, and ratios could predict newspaper consolidation beyond chance. He reported that discrepant circulations in sister dailies would result in the demise of the paper with less circulation.

After much debate and research evidence, the conclusion reached is the same as that presented by Udell (1978). Chain ownership has the potential of either improving or decreasing the journalistic product, but certainly there is no consistent documentation that group ownership of newspapers is inherently bad. The chief changes likely to occur with chain ownership are related to economic considerations, primarily:

> Chains have a distinct economic advantage derived from their experience and expertise in management, marketing and use of the economies of scale. Evidence is that this financial planning sophistication can make newspapers more profitable businesses without debasing the journalistic product.

REFERENCES

Demographics of Newsroom Personnel

Epstein, E. J. (1973). *News from nowhere.* New York: Random House.
Gans, H. J. (1979). *Deciding what's news.* New York: Pantheon Books.
Gans, H. J. (1985, November/December). Are U.S. journalists dangerously liberal? *Columbia Journalism Review,* pp. 29-30.
Johnstone, J.W.C., Slawski, E. J., & Bowman, W. W. (1976). *The news people: A sociological portrait of American journalists and their work.* Urbana: University of Illinois Press.
Lichter, L., Lichter, S. R., & Rothman, S. (1982, December). The once and future journalist. *Washington Journalism Review,* pp. 26-27.
Lichter, S. R., & Rothman, S. (1981, October/November). Media and business ethics. *Public Opinion,* pp. 42-46, 59-60.
Schwed, W. W. (1981). Hiring, promotion, salary, longevity trends charted at dailies. *Newspaper Research Journal, 3*(1), 3.
Sigal, L. V. (1973). *Reporters and officials: The organization and politics of newsmaking.* Lexington, MA: D. C. Heath.
Tuchman, G. (1978). *Making news.* New York: Pantheon Books.
Weaver, D. H., & Wilhoit, G. C. (1986). *The American journalists: A portrait of U.S. news people and their work.* Bloomington: Indiana University Press.

Salaries, Women, and Minorities

American Society of Newspaper Editors. (1984). *1984 Report.* Washington, DC: Author.
Davis, J., & Westmoreland, R. (1974). Minority editorial workers on Texas daily newspapers. *Journalism Quarterly, 51,* 132-134.
Guimary, D. L. (1984). Ethnic minorities in newsrooms of major market media in California. *Journalism Quarterly, 61,* 827-830.
Johnstone, J.W.C., Slawski, E. J., & Bowman, W. W. (1976). *The news people: A sociological portrait of American journalists and their work.* Urbana: University of Illinois Press.
Jurney, D. (1980, December/January). Women are creeping into policymaking jobs on U.S. newspapers. *ASNE Bulletin,* p. 14.
Ogan, C. L. (1980). On their way to the top? Men and women middle-level newspaper managers. *Newspaper Research Journal, 1*(3), 51.

Ogan, C. L. (1983). Life at the top for men and women newspaper managers: A five-year update of their characteristics. *Newspaper Research Journal, 5*(2), 57.

Ogan, C. L., & Weaver, D. H. (1979, April). Women in newspaper management: A contradiction in terms? *Newspaper Research Journal* [prototype], 42.

Sohn, A. B. (1981). Women in newspaper management: An update. *Newspaper Research Journal, 3*(1), 94.

Sohn, A. B. (1984). Goals and achievement orientations of women newspaper managers. *Journalism Quarterly, 61,* 600-605.

Trayes, E. J. (1969). The Negro in journalism: Surveys show low ratios. *Journalism Quarterly, 46,* 5-8.

Trayes, E. J. (1979) "Black journalists on U.S. metropolitan daily newspapers: A follow-up study. *Journalism Quarterly,* 711-714.

Wilson, J. G. (1981, March). You love the work—But how soon will you starve? *Washington Journalism Review,* pp. 12-17.

Hiring, Training, and Continuing Education

Barwis, G. L. (1978, August). Contractual newsroom democracy. *Journalism Monographs, No.* 57.

Chusmir, L. H. (1983). Profile of motivational needs of individuals in the newspaper industry. *Newspaper Research Journal, 5*(1), 33.

Fedler, F., & Taylor, P. (1981). Reporters and the Newspaper Guild: Membership attitudes and salaries. *Journalism Quarterly, 58,* 83-88.

Johnstone, J.W.C., Slawski, E. J., & Bowman, W. W. (1976). *The news people: A sociological portrait of American journalists and their work.* Urbana: University of Illinois Press.

Joseph, T. (1983). A study of alcohol use by reporters and editors. *Newspaper Research Journal, 4*(2), 3.

Ogan, C. L. (1980). On their way to the top? Men and women middle-level newspaper managers. *Newspaper Research Journal, 1*(3), 51.

Ogan, C. L. (1983). Life at the top for men and women newspaper managers: A five-year update of their characteristics. *Newspaper Research Journal, 5*(2), 57.

Ogan, C. L., & Weaver, D. H. (1979, April). Women in newspaper management: A contradiction in terms? *Newspaper Research Journal,* [Prototype], 42.

Pease, T. (1986). Back to the newsroom: Journalism educators' professional activities. *Newspaper Research Journal, 7*(2), 39.

Smith, R. (1982). Employment screening procedures: Tests and tryouts. *Newspaper Research Journal, 3*(2), 27.

Sohn, A. B., & Chusmir, L. H. (1985). The motivational perspectives of newspaper managers. *Journalism Quarterly, 62,* 296-303.

Trayes, E. J. (1976). Hiring and promotion practices: A survey of 52 APME dailies. *Journalism Quarterly, 53,* 540-544.

Vannatta, B. A. (1981). Hemisphericity and journalism—How do journalists think? *Newspaper Research Journal, 3*(1), 9.

Management-Style Considerations

American Society of Newspaper Editors Foundation. (1985). *Newsroom management handbook.* Washington, DC: Author.

Barwis, G. L. (1978, August). Contractual newsroom democracy. *Journalism Monographs, No. 57.*

Bennett, D. (1985). Editors as managers: Their perceived need for specialized training. *Newspaper Research Journal, 6*(4), 24.

Burgoon, J. K., Bernstein, J. M, Burgoon, M., & Atkin, C. K. (1984). Journalists' perceptions of the future of the newspaper industry. *Newspaper Research Journal, 5*(3), 13.

Burgoon, J., Burgoon, M., & Atkin, C. (1982). *The world of the working journalist.* New York: Newspaper Advertising Bureau.

Flatt, D. M. (1980). Managerial incentives: Effects at a chain-owned daily. *Newspaper Research Journal, 2*(1), 48.

Fowler, G. L., & Shipman, J. M. (1984). Pennsylvania editors' perceptions of communication in the newsroom. *Journalism Quarterly, 61,* 822-826.

Johnstone, J.W.C., Slawski, E. J., & Bowman, W. W. (1976). *The news people: A sociological portrait of American journalists and their work.* Urbana: University of Illinois Press.

Joseph, T. (1981). Existing decision-making practices on American dailies. *Newspaper Research Journal, 2*(4), 56.

Joseph, T. (1982a). Decision-making preferences and practices. *Newspaper Research Journal, 3*(3), 37.

Joseph, T. (1982b). Reporters' and editors' preference toward reporter decision-making. *Journalism Quarterly, 59,* 219-222, 284.

Kaufman, J. A. (1981). Effectiveness of bilateral and unilateral newspaper administrative structure. *Newspaper Research Journal 3*(1), 54.

Pettus, A. (1981). Commentary: Peer review: *The Tennessean's* innovative experiment. *Newspaper Research Journal, 2*(4), 89.

Rucker, F. W., & Williams, H. L. (1955). *Newspaper organization and management.* Ames: Iowa State University Press.

Sohn, A., Ogan, C., & Polich, J. (1986). *Newspaper leadership.* Englewood Cliffs, NJ: Prentice-Hall.

Trayes, E. J. (1978). Managing editors and their newsrooms: A survey of 208 APME members. *Journalism Quarterly, 55,* 744-749, 898.

Weaver, D. H., & Wilhoit, G. C. (1986). *The American journalist: A portrait of U.S. news people and their work.* Bloomington: Indiana University Press.

Ziter, C. B. (1981). Commentary: More effective people management through QWL. *Newspaper Research Journal, 2*(3), 64.

The Weight of Chains

Becker, L. B., Beam, R., & Russial, J. (1978). Correlates of daily newspaper performance in New England. *Journalism Quarterly, 55,* 100-108.

Blankenburg, W. B. (1982). Newspaper ownership and control of circulation to increase profits. *Journalism Quarterly, 59,* 390-398.

Blankenburg, W. B. (1983). A newspaper chain's pricing behavior. *Journalism Quarterly, 60,* 275-280.

Blankenburg, W. B. (1985). Consolidation in two-newspaper firms. *Journalism Quarterly, 62,* 474-481.

Browning, N., Grierson, D., & Howard, H. H. (1984). Effects of conglomerate takeover on a newspaper's coverage of the Knoxville World's Fair: A case study. *Newspaper Research Journal, 6*(1), 30.

Commission on Freedom of the Press. (1947). *A free and responsible press*. Chicago: Univerity of Chicago Press.

Dertouzos, J. N., & Thorpe, K. E. (1982). *Newspaper groups: Economics of scale, tax laws, and merger incentives*. Santa Monica, CA: Rand.

Donohue, G. A., Olien, C. N., & Tichenor, P. J. (1985). Reporting conflict by pluralism, newspaper type, and ownership. *Journalism Quarterly, 62*, 489-499, 507.

Lacy, S. (1985). Monopoly metropolitan dailies and inter-city competition. *Journalism Quarterly, 62*, 640-644.

McGrath, K., & Gaziano, C. (1986). Dimensions of media credibility: Highlights of the 1985 ASNE survey. *Newspaper Research Journal, 7*(2), 55.

Pasadeos, Y. (1984). Application of measures of sensationalism to a Murdoch-owned daily in the San Antonio market. *Newspaper Research Journal, 5*(4), 9.

Rarick, G., & Hartman, B. (1966). The effects of competition on one daily newspaper's content. *Journalism Quarterly, 43*, 459-463.

Schweitzer, J. D., & Goldman, E. (1975). Does newspaper competition make a difference to readers? Journalism Quarterly, 52, 706-710.

Soloski, J. (1979). Economics and management. The real influence of newspaper groups. *Newspaper Research Journal, 1*: 1-19.

Stempel, G. H., III. (1966). A new analysis of monopoly and competition: Daily newspapers' content. *Journalism Quarterly, 43*, 459-463.

Stempel, G. H., III. (1973, June). Effects on performance of a cross-media monopoly. *Journalism Monographs, No. 29*.

Stone, G. C., Stone, D. B., & Trotter, E. P. (1981). Newspaper quality's relation to circulation. *Newspaper Research Journal, 2*(3), 16.

Tillinghast, W. A. (1984). Slanting the news: Source perceptions after changes in newspaper management. *Journalism Quarterly, 61*, 310-316.

Udell, J. G. (1978). *The economics of the American newspaper* (pp. 75-77). New York: Hastings House.

5

AUDIENCE ATTENTION TO NEWSPAPERS

Newspapers are dependent on audience acceptance, and while this is one of the most extensive research areas, it is also the industry's least integrated area of research.

Newspaper managers have been concerned with their audience since the industry became a mass medium. The clearer it became that a newspaper's market success depended on public acceptance, the more interest managers took in their reading audiences. Newspaper research followed the same pattern. In the earliest stages of newspaper research, the reading public was given little attention. When the audience was mentioned, the reference usually was to an amorphous group of newspaper buyers or readers. Until the 1940s, the newspaper audience was not recognized formally in the research as being composed first of groups and second of individuals.

Yet early research—in fact most early writings about newspapers—did contain references to the newspaper-reading habit.

THE NEWSPAPER-READING HABIT

The habitual aspect of newspaper use is one of the less-than-fully-explored central themes of newspaper research. It's unclear if the topic received short shrift because reading habits were assumed a truism or because studying habits seemed to offer little of practical value. But recent studies of the habitual nature of newspaper use very definitely confirm its existence.

The Newspaper Advertising Bureau (NAB), in a series of research reports, charted how individuals grow into their mass media patterns. In fact, the entire range of newspaper readership studies—literally thousands of surveys as well as more sophisticated research strategies during the past 30 years—yields the following scenario of how people develop their newspaper-reading habits.

(1) Young children, prior to first grade or as soon as they learn to read, begin perusing the color Sunday comics section and look at weekday comics.

Obviously, a newspaper has to be available to children at home if such experimentation is to occur.

(2) From ages 6 to about 10 children begin looking at other content; and by about age 12 boys begin reading sports and girls begin reading advice columns and sports. By age 12 or 13, many children will be scanning news with at least some degree of regularity.

(3) The newspaper-reading habit begins in earnest during the high school years. Here the choice of daily reading can be made. High-school-aged youngsters establish (or don't establish) a newspaper-reading pattern that approaches adult readership. By their late teens, youngsters' content interests and reading frequency patterns are almost set for the rest of their lives.

(4) In their young adult years, ages 18 to 24, those who have not already begun a newspaper-reading habit might change dramatically. While it's likely newspaper use will decrease for some young adult readers, the preponderance for change will be toward increased newspaper use.

(5) The 18- to 24-year-old period involves the greatest life-style changes. Whereas being single and away from home in college are related to lessened newspaper use, being married, starting a household, and beginning a family are associated with higher newspaper use. By the time young adults reach their late 20s, their newspaper habits are in place.

(6) Patterns remain fixed through the 55- to 65-year-old range. But, reading frequency drops slightly after age 65, due possibly to health, eyesight, or finances.

For the mass reading audience, the habitual nature of newspaper use is a well-established quantity. Recent research shows even more evidence of habits at play. Stone and Wetherington (1979) surveyed a small sample of college students in California and found a strong correlation between a college student's present newspaper use and the way the student remembered parents using the newspaper while the student was growing up at home. Findings showed: (1) Among students who said their parents had been regular newspaper readers, 69% were reading a paper three or more days a week, but the figure was only 49% for those whose parents were not regular newspaper readers; (2) if parents had a special time to read the newspaper, so did students; (3) if parents had a special place to read the paper, so did students; (4) students were likely to read the newspaper at the same time of day their parents did; and (5) students were currently likely to read the newspaper in the same room they remembered their parents having read it. The authors concluded:

Newspaper reading is so strong an habitual practice—manifest through repetitive actions—even college students are bound by those newspaper reading habits they established at home perhaps 10 years earlier.

The contrast is even more striking when it is remembered these college students were in that 18- to-24-year-old age group experiencing their most independent life-styles. They were continuing their parents' reading habits when their parents' life-styles were most established. The study was replicated (Stone & Windhauser, 1983) in two Southern university towns on a sample of 800 students with the same results prevailing. A recent study by the NAB (1984) showed dramatic life-style changes, such as moving or marriage, result in jolting the newspaper-reading habit. Stamm (1985) found newcomers to a community often experience a lapse in subscribing. Stone (1986) and Rarick and Lemert (1986) demonstrated the entire range of an audience's mass media habits can change dramatically when a newspaper moves from a P.M. to an A.M. publishing cycle. Although research clearly demonstrates the habitual nature of newspaper use, it has not yet been exploited by the newspaper industry. Newspaper researchers know little about how habits are established, what causes them to be altered, or what marketing strategies might be employed to increase the readership base. Still, this macro approach to investigating the newspaper use habit is relatively new (Gollin, 1985). There are micro approaches—focusing primarily on reader demographics—that have yielded substantial rewards and from which the industry mines benefits.

DEMOGRAPHICS AND PSYCHOGRAPHICS

Instead of viewing the mass audience as a single unit, newspaper industry researchers have followed the best tactics of marketing experts who subdivided audiences into similar groups. Once the audience is segmented into groups with common traits, it is possible to redesign aspects of the product so that it will have more appeal to target audience segments. The newspaper industry has followed this strategy for about 30 years, with varying degrees of success.

Age, Education, Income, and Race

Very little in the entire realm of mass communication research is as certain as this single finding:

Older, more educated and higher income individuals are the most likely newspaper clients.

Virtually every study of newspaper readership supports the finding, over a period of 40 years (Schramm & White, 1947). While there certainly will be individual exceptions—some young, less-educated, and poorer people are frequent newspaper readers—this overall finding will prevail. Minor refinements also prevail. For instance, the drop-off in readership for those over age 65 (Salisbury, 1981) has already been noted. Likewise, it should be clear that income and education are two closely linked demographics: People with more educational attainment are likely to have higher income. Studies differ in attributing more importance to education or income when these two variables are considered independently. Differences are also noted in studies that combine multiple independent variables and in the statistical approaches used (Gollin, 1985). As Tipton (1978) noted in his summary of recent readership findings, "The demographics of readership are relatively consistent and have been. . . . Readers are older, more highly educated and have higher incomes."

In studies of race as a readership predictor, virtually all findings indicate minorities—and most research has dealt specifically with blacks as a large and growing minority—are less likely to be newspaper readers than whites. Of course minorities are more likely to fall into the nonreader category based on the other demographics as well (NAB, 1978): They are likely to have less educational attainment, to be in lower socioeconomic groups, and to be younger (since this is an increasing racial group). Bogart (1981) presents the case made by other researchers that blacks are not represented on newspaper editorial staffs and their interests are not well represented in the news content of newspapers.

Additionally, a study by Jackson (1978) showed blacks' readership patterns are highly similar to whites' when minorities are segmented demographically: Older, better-educated blacks rely more on the newspaper than their younger, less-educated counterparts. A recent study (Freidman, 1985) found that when blacks are matched demographically with whites, newspaper-readership levels for blacks are even higher than those for whites. On the question of race:

> Blacks have been found not to read newspapers with the same degree of frequency as whites, but there is evidence this group may become (or be encouraged to become) a more significant client for newspapers.

Male Versus Female Reading

Sex has been another demographic variable used to segment the newspaper-reading audience. Newspaper content traditionally has been differentiated into topics assumed to appeal to one sex or the other: cooking, sports, fashion, advice, business. Early research focused on the differences in interests—and found them. For instance, sports readers were more likely to be male; advice readers were more likely to be female. As research became more sophisticated, society's concept of traditional differentiation in behavior by sex waned, and the focus of research attention shifted to readership similarities rather than differences. The similarities were documented as well.

In fact, the prevailing finding today is that sex is a weak predictor of newspaper-reading traits.

> Women comprise the majority of readership for advice columns, fashion and food sections, display ads and coupons. Men comprise the majority of readership for sports and business. But men and women do read content traditionally regarded as the other sex's domain. The overlap in readership for some of these categories is extensive. Editors should approach all decisions about content from the standpoint it is being read by members of both sexes.

Recent distinctions found by audience sex are that men's reading interests tend to be more focused than women's and men may be more selective than women in content read (Gollin, 1985). Also, men read the newspaper more times during a day than do women. Weaver (1978) found patterns of newspaper-material readership different for men and women. Whereas men read straight-news items then editorials and columns, then features and entertainment; women read editorials and columns, then entertainment, then straight-news items and listings. But the Weaver study concluded readership levels by content items was highly similar for men and women. Even in the area of coupon clipping, the traditional view that it's a woman's habit is wrong. Winter and DeGeorge (1980) found 61% of female respondents said they clip coupons regularly, and 57% of male respondents said they did. Einsiedel and Tully (1981) reviewed four studies and found no consistent distinctions could be made between readership patterns of working and nonworking women. However, an eight-year comparison study by the Newspaper Advertising Bureau (1979) showed working women were more frequent newspaper readers than nonworking women, and those who worked gave higher interest ratings to a much wider variety of content than those who didn't. And Johnson and Gross (1985) found women in decision-making positions use newspapers more and use media more for professional and work-related information.

The suggestion is that as women become more involved in the workplace, their newspaper-reading patterns will more closely match those of men. Hence, the distinctions in content interests traditionally attributed to sex will continue to disappear.

BEYOND RAW DEMOGRAPHICS

The search for reader demographic differences that might explain newspaper use was not successful. While it was possible to segment the mass audience into subsets that paid more and less attention to newspapers, the industry was provided little usable information on which to make content decisions. The demographic variables used (age, education, income, and sex) were simply too gross to be acted upon meaningfully. Another approach was needed and was provided by newspaper researchers. However, whereas the key demographic variables were flawed by their simplicity, the move into more sophisticated readership predictors is flawed by its complexity. At least four areas of personal attributes have received extensive research: community involvement, psychographics, public affairs interest, and the duty to keep informed. Study-for-study, there has been more work in the personal attitudes and behaviors area than in the older key demographics area. The extent of study was logged by Poindexter (1978) who found more than 100 new research findings in what has possibly been the single newspaper research growth area of the last decade. The great range and depth of these studies prevents more than a very general overview.

Community Involvement

In his review of correlates with newspaper circulation, Stone (1978) identified owner-occupied households, length of residence, and individual social interaction in the community as strong predictors of newspaper use. His (1977) theory of community commitment was based on an index showing stronger attachment to the community was associated with higher levels of newspaper circulation in the community. Of course "community commitment" is related as well with demographics of individuals that have been consistently associated with higher newspaper readership: People in their mid-life stages who have greater income (they own their homes) are likely to be married and have school-aged children. All of these demographics are linked to greater life-style stability and social interaction with neighbors, the schools and churches, and community organizations.

> People who are solidly established in the community are the best clients for newspapers. Their interests are closely associated with the content newspapers provide.

Stephens (1978) found adults with strong community attachments spend more time with newspapers than those with weaker community attachments. People with strong community attachments make more recommendations about changing newspaper format and content, and their recommendations for change deal with community rather than personal content items. Those with multiple-community attachments—related to their mobility—are more likely to read more than one newspaper. The feeling of attachment to the community is more predictive of newspaper reading than a person's age, years of residence in the community, socioeconomic status, income, or education.

Stevenson (1979) extended the community ties concept by identifying a traditional newspaper audience "with strong, permanent bonds to the community, whose need for information, guidance and community surveillance leads to reading hard news, editorials and background features." This survey documented that people who were more likely to vote in local elections, have an interest in local politics and say they expected to be in the community the next five years, thought "keeping in touch with the community" was a very important reason for reading a newspaper. Becker, Collins, and Fruit (1980) found newspaper non-readers and skimmers were less motivated to keep up with what was happening in their communities and the nation. Stamm (1981) looked at community *involvement,* defined as activity with organized groups, and *identification,* defined as a feeling of belonging to the community. Involvement by itself had little relationship to greater newspaper use, but in combination with identification the two measures were related to subscribing to several newspapers and to spending more time reading. This research also showed that more reliance on newspapers was related to people's feeling of community identification.

Shaw and Fortini-Campbell (1978) showed that in small towns the newspaper is considered a vital link to local and political happenings. "Small-town residents are faithful readers of their local newspaper for local and non-local news," the researchers reported and noted as well that a small-town daily newspaper, particularly one located far from a larger metropolitan area, has virtually no competition for the news it provides.

Jackson (1982) found residents moving to the suburbs had strong attachments to the suburbs as a way of life. They rated their suburban newspaper higher than their metropolitan paper on: taking strong stands on controversial issues, openness to personal opinions or views, raising important issues or problems, carrying advertisements of stores shopped at, concern about people and their problems, and active support for community projects.

> The research on community attachment and newspaper use indicates a person's identification with his or her community is related to how the newspaper will be used. "Use" includes frequency, reliance, attitude toward the paper and content preferences.

Psychographics

Community attachment considerations are related at least tangentially to the area of research called *psychographics,* or *readers' psychological life-styles.* Through sophisticated factor-analysis computer programs, survey respondents' answers to a number of questions are compared to determine if those answers can be grouped into similar categories. For instance, some newspaper readers may consider weather, stocks, international news, and sports their most important interest items and may give high ratings to these content items. Others may rate television listings, advice columns, and comics as their content priorities. A researcher looking at these results might consider the first type of reader "news" hounds; the second "entertainment" enthusiasts. The researcher would then select and describe the traits of news hounds, comparing those traits with traits of entertainment enthusiasts.

While this concocted example may sound simple, the procedure is almost always much more complex since answers don't group so neatly. The researcher is usually faced with making compromises. Further complications occur since the dimensions established by answers to one study are not likely to be equivalent with dimensions established by another: The same dimensions rarely are reported between any two studies. Even with these major drawbacks, psychographic studies yield general insights that seem to be consistent over time and can be acted upon by newspaper decision makers. Meyer (1982) demonstrated how psychographics can be used to describe newspaper readers' life-styles and distinguish A.M. and P.M. readers in different newspaper markets. His groups were called seekers, adventurers, worriers, and watchers. Each group was identified by its demographic traits. Knowing these traits and how their newspapers were appealing to each group, editors could make market decisions to improve content appeal for the lower-interest reader types.

Schweitzer (1977) reviewed studies of life-style and readership. Westley and Severin (1964) found newspaper readers could be distinguished from nonreaders since nonreaders were less active in community and church affairs, were geographically and socially isolated and tended to rely on other people for information. Kline (1971) found using life-style data in conjunction with demographic data was a better predictor of time people spend with different media during the week than relying solely on demographic data for this information. Bryant, Currier, and Morrison (1976) used the life-style distinction to describe a newspaper's present readers, determine what content appeals to them, and what content might appeal to current nonreaders. Mauro and

Weaver (1977) found four types of reading patterns: current events, sports, personal entertainment, and service. These readership patterns were distinct: reading one category of content was not related to reading the other categories.

Larkin, Grotta, and Stout (1977) found young adults' differing life-styles make them less newspaper oriented. The life-styles analysis showed those in the 21- to 34-year-old age group have a view toward newspapers and the kinds of content they'd like to see in newspapers entirely different from that of older adults. The researchers offered a variety of content change suggestions editors might use to make the newspaper more appealing to this age group's interests.

Burgoon and Burgoon (1981) did an analysis of public expectations of newspapers in five different markets. Expectations found, in their order of importance to readers, were (1) immediacy and thoroughness, (2) local awareness and utility, (3) redundancy and entertainment, and (4) social extension or gossip. These expectations were generally the same for all age groups in all markets. Although there were some differences noted by other demographic breakdowns—education, sex, income, readership frequency, or residence proximity to the metro-politan market studied—the difference patterns were minor, indicating newspaper content expectations are not highly dependent on demo-graphics. In addition, the researchers found these same content expectations for television news, indicating "television news is perceived along the same function lines as newspaper news."

A similar approach was reported by Schwartz, Moore, and Krekel (1979) who found four types of newspaper readers: young optimists, accounting for about 18% of the sample; traditional conservatives, 31%; progressive conservatives, 37%; and grim independents, 15%. These factor labels are merely umbrella terms. For instance, the "young optimists" label was derived from questionnaire answers such as "My greatest achievements are ahead of me" and "I like to be a little different from others." Yet it is possible to segment a market's audience into these life-style types and look at their newspaper content preferences. The researchers said psychographic studies can help marketing executives position the newspaper as a product among readers, help editors understand how readers use specific parts of the newspaper, and explain the newspaper-use process in human terms.

The best value of psychographic studies is their ability to give editors and marketing executives an overview of the whole newspaper market. Instead of focusing only on age or race, these more sophisticated studies group people by their interests, needs and habits. While there are significant problems in methodology and interpretation, this research procedure gives newspaper managers their best view of the reading audience.

If reader types were studied by relying solely on demographics, much of the rich underpinnings of what is taking place would be lost. The market might be conceptualized in a grossly simplistic and inaccurate way. For instance, Poindexter (1978) isolated typical nonreaders (low income, the youngest and oldest adults, low education) and *atypical* nonreaders (those whose higher income and education demographics indicated they should be newspaper readers). She found two-thirds of the atypical nonreaders said they avoid newspapers because of the content. Only about one-third of the typical nonreaders mentioned content as a reason they avoid newspapers.

Public Affairs Interests

Another area of newspaper research that goes beyond raw demographic data is a person's interest in politics or public affairs. The area is both old and new, as the assumption, since Lippmann's early writing, is that people more interested in politics and political affairs are better newspaper readers: They read papers more frequently and they read more portions of the paper, including the opinion pages. The new aspect is that only recently has serious attention been paid to implications of political interest on newspaper reading—how greatly reading is affected by a person's interest in public affairs.

Countless studies verified newspaper reading is closely related to a person's interest in public affairs. Kebbel (1985) looked at a 1979 national survey by the Institute of Survey Research at Temple University. He found political activity closely associated with newspaper readership. The association remained with age and education being held constant.

Smith used national election survey data from 1972, 1976, and 1980. He reported newspaper readership relates strongly to both political knowledge and activity. Smith wrote, "Newspaper readership is itself a major determinant of political activity and . . . this relationship has remained constant over time" (1986: 53). Smith found there was no associated relationship between a person's interest in politics and viewing political news on television. The study also determined the association between political knowledge and activity remained strong at different levels of social class and education. While Kebbel and Smith found demographics did not influence the relationship between political interest and readership, most studies have noted people's interest in public affairs is closely associated with demographics such as age, education, and income. McLeod and Choe (1978) found "a minimal level of political interest seems to be a crucial element distinguishing those who read a newspaper at least occasionally from those who never read." However, political interest did not discriminate infrequent from frequent reading, nor did it discriminate single-paper readers from multiple-paper readers. Further, in a scale developed to determine an individual's perceived duty to keep informed, higher scale scores were closely associated with education, income, and age.

Duty to Keep Informed

A detailed analysis of the strength of civic attitude and its influence on newspaper use was provided in a special edition of *Newspaper Research Journal* (1983). A scale of civic attitude was developed that consisted of responses to the following four opinion items: (1) We all have a duty to keep ourselves informed about news and current events; (2) it is important to be informed about news and current events; (3) so many other people follow the news and keep informed about it that it doesn't matter much whether I do or not; and (4) a good deal of news about current events isn't important enough to keep informed about.

The more strongly a person feels a duty to keep informed, the more likely that person is to be a client for newspapers.

McCombs (1983) reported that as scores on the scale increased, the proportion of daily readers increased monotonically: The stronger a person's duty to keep informed, the more likely that person was to be a frequent newspaper reader. The perceived duty was associated also with higher national television news viewing. The duty was not related strongly with weekly newspaper use or with local television and radio news use.

Weaver and Fielder (1983) reported findings from a study of Chicago metropolitan and suburban dwellers. Here civic attitudes in conjunction with demographics were related to reading a metro paper by suburbanites. The scale did not predict metro paper reading for metropolitan residents; "reading a metropolitan newspaper as a city resident is a routine behavior that cuts across different social classes and levels of civic attitudes," the researchers reported.

In an effort to separate civic attitude from demographics, Olsen (1983) reported the association between strength of feeling a duty to keep informed and news exposure "is positive and significant, and not due to underlying differences in demographic characteristics of respondents." The more strongly a person felt a civic duty to keep informed, the more likely that person was to be a frequent newspaper reader. And, the perceived duty was associated with higher national television news viewing. The duty was not related strongly with weekly newspaper use or with local television and radio news use.

Einsiedel and Kang (1983) used the civic attitudes scale to determine if it predicted reading or subscribing. The researchers found both measures of newspaper use were related to a person's self-perceived duty to keep informed. But the duty was more closely associated with reading a newspaper than with subscribing to one. The finding suggests feeling a duty to keep informed is a motivator for single-copy buying.

Three other studies, all from the special edition of *Newspaper Research Journal,* showed that the duty to keep informed predicted newspaper readership in Hawaii, in Sweden, and among recent emigrants from the Soviet Union. Hence civic attitude can be considered a universal correlate with newspaper readership.

In all, research studies that go beyond raw demographics show audience behavior, life-styles, interests, and opinions are more sophisticated ways of describing people's attention to newspapers than demographic variables of age, education, income, and sex. While demographics are significant and do relate to readership, the demographic approach is enhanced when more complex behavioral variables are added. In fact, the behavioral variables often supersede raw demographics as a method of explaining audience attention and use of newspapers.

APPLICATION WITH YOUNG READERS

The decline in newspaper use among young adults serves as an example of a knotty readership problem researchers have been grappling with since the mid-1970s. Industry researchers had noted that between 1967 and 1974, the penetration of newspapers for all adults 18 and over dropped from 76% to 72.3%, a net decline of about 4%. During the same period, penetration among young adults—those 18-24 years old—had dropped from 71% to 61%, a net decline of 10%. The loss was estimated to have cost the newspaper industry about 2.5 million readers daily. More frightening was the possibility of a trend: Younger readers might continue to turn away from newspapers every ensuing year until the entire adult market had been eroded.

Rather than reacting to the symptom, the industry tried to treat the cause by finding out why young adults weren't reading a daily newspaper. Losing its young adult readers prompted the industry's first major research undertaking with funding at several levels by a variety of organizations. One of the earlier major studies was funded by Harte Hanks (Yankelovich, Skelly, & White, 1976) and used the focus group approach to separately interview young people and editors, although this was only one of hundreds of projects undertaken.

The general line of reasoning was:

(1) The problem could be temporary. Young adults might be turning away from newspapers because of Vietnam, the Arab oil embargo, the cultural revolution, Watergate, or drugs. If temporary, the problem will disappear as soon as these conditions change.

Unfortunately, the "temporary" explanation lost ground when readership declines for older adults (which had also been occurring) stabilized in 1973-1974, but losses for younger adults continued.

(2) The problem could be related to young people's life-styles. Some possible specifics are (a) lack of time to read, (b) more working women, and (c) young adults are more unsettled.

Two of these explanations were discarded. While it is true "lack of time" is the reason most frequently given by people who don't read the newspaper, research studies show people—at every age—who have the most active daily life-styles are also more likely to be newspaper readers. Likewise, working women are among the most active individuals, and working women were found to be more frequent newspaper readers than nonworking women at every age level.

The third explanation, that young adults are more unsettled, had some support from current census data about the 18- to 24-year-old age category, For instance, there was a declining marriage rate, and young people were waiting longer before getting married. Between 1960 and 1975, the percentage of unmarried young adult males increased 7% to about 60% of all males in the category; young unmarried females increased 12% to about 40% of all females in the category. There were more childless couples in the 20- to 24-year-old age range. In 1965 only 28% of the married couples were childless; by 1975 the figure had climbed to 43%. There were increases in divorce rates, mobility, and apartment-house living. All of these census figures showed young adults were more rootless. Rootlessness results in delaying formation of family units, and family units are the basis of the strongest commitment to newspaper reading.

But none of the census figures shows a substantial enough change to account for all the lost readership among young adults. In combination, however, the figures do indicate young people are more unsettled than their peers of earlier generations, and the net effect could account for much of the lost readership in this age cohort. One view would be that newspaper readership among these young adults will increase as they become more settled. Another view is their life-styles are so different from those of previous generations that even becoming more settled will not bring their readership level up to that of their older counterparts. When this readership project began, very little was known about how unsettledness affected newspaper use. The industry could not gamble that young adults would return to newspapers when they became more settled.

(3) Competing mass media, particularly television, accounted for the loss of young newspaper readers. Faced with the first real television generation—people who had television since their infancy—newspapers ceased to be the attraction they had been for previous generations.

Numerous studies have shown how much public confidence in—and reliance on—television news has increased since its inception. People report they get their news more frequently from TV and would believe it over conflicting reports in newspapers. Television news offerings have increased from 15 minutes to half an hour on the national networks, and local stations have gone to half-hour and one-hour formats. Television news is considered more personal than newspapers, and video reports provide the "seeing is believing" effect.

While many in the newspaper industry considered television the chief culprit in stealing young readers, research showed differently. Young adults were found to be no more heavily dependent on television than older adults. When young adults were divided into heavy and light television viewers, no differences were found in newspaper readership levels between the two groups. Finally, for the mass audience, people who watch television news also are likely to read a newspaper. These findings strongly suggest television was not the culprit.

(4) Young adults are unable to read a newspaper. They either do not possess the necessary reading skills or they find reading a chore instead of a pleasurable activity.

It is true that in the mid-1970s national standardized tests of high school students' English abilities were showing dramatically lower scores than those achieved by the previous generation. There was a national debate about the level of learning taking place in elementary and secondary education.

While reading levels offered a plausible explanation for the loss of young adult newspaper readers, there was simply too much evidence on the other side. Young adults were buying a disproportionately large share of paperback books and were reading special interest magazines and "underground" newspapers. In some cities where test scores showed low reading levels, local newspapers had a large share of young adult readers. Also, the 18- to 24-year-old group being studied was much more likely to have completed high school and to have attended or graduated college than young adults in the previous generation. In all, any real lack of reading skills (whether they had dropped is debatable) did not seem to account for the loss in young adult newspaper readers.

(5) There is something about the newspaper itself that has become a turn-off for young adults.

Ruling out many of the other possibilities left the likelihood that the newspaper's appeal to young adults had waned. In fact, the research seemed to show this is what had happened. First, newspapers were found to have an image problem among young adults who saw reading the newspaper: (1) as an "old people's habit . . . something you see old people do while waiting for a bus," (2) as speaking for the status quo and being against change in the society, (3) as being cold and impersonal, and (4) as a middle-aged product written and edited by middle-aged people for a middle-aged audience. Additionally, content was found not to appeal to young adults who noted the newspaper carried stock market quotations and politics but not records or outdoor roller skating. The newspaper was said not to be covering the "me" generation—the more individualistic, self-improvement concerns of young adults.

In addition to content, young adults offered several negatives about how the newspaper looks. Among complaints were newspapers are bulky and reading them is work; the type is small, the physical pages are large and cumbersome, there are too many jumps; sentences are too long; things aren't put together in the same place; indexing is poor; and the layout is dull.

The major outcome of research on eroding readership among young adults was that the newspaper was no longer appealing to this audience segment as it had in the past. The problem was with newspapers. They had not properly anticipated changing reader interests and had not changed.

In fairness to industry practices—and to concede that even a massive research effort is likely to derive conflicting findings—some of the research indicated the decline in young readers was overstated: It really wasn't a crisis for the industry. Some of the research also showed younger adults generally want the same things from newspapers that older adults want. Critics cautioned remaking newspapers to appeal to younger adults might jeopardize older adults' commitment. Others believed the losses in readership could be stemmed through a better marketing effort to convince young adults that the newspaper does meet their interests.

In the 10 years from 1975 to 1985, the industry continued its attention on research about young adults' interests, needs, life-styles, and newspaper readership. Great strides were made in using the new printing technologies, in makeup and design, indexing, humanizing stories, providing analysis, and adding columns and features for young adults. In all, through the research findings and industry efforts, declining readership among young adults did stabilize in the mid-1980s, although this segment of the population still has the lowest percentage of newspaper readers among all adults.

THE ACTIVE INDIVIDUAL

A side benefit of readership research—both the recent research on young adults and previous readership studies—is a consistent confirmation of the "active individual." While no new theory has been offered to this effect, studies show:

People who read newspapers are also engaged in many other activities. They are involved in their community. They feel a duty to keep informed. They are more likely to be politically active and knowledgeable about public affairs. They are likely to keep up with the "news" generally, both through newspapers and television news.

The demographic information also shows readers are likely to be better educated and have higher incomes. Those of ages 35 to 55 are likely to be the most committed readers. Those who have lived in the community for several years and who intend to continue living there for several more, are also likely to be committed readers. And people whose children are in school are also more likely to be newspaper readers.

In all, the picture is an unusually bright one for newspapers. Audience members who are likely to be opinion leaders—influentials and stalwarts in the community—are those most committed to reading newspapers. They are also likely to be people in leadership positions, those with the most spendable income, and those who are active doers. They are the people advertisers and editors want to reach most, and it is apparent newspapers reach them consistently. While the industry would certainly prefer 80% penetration among all audience segments over age 18, if such a level never can be achieved again, at least the penetration level continues to be among the most desirable segment of the entire audience.

REFERENCES

The Newspaper Reading Habit

Bogart, L. (1981). *Press and public: Who reads what, when, where, and why in American newspapers.* Hillsdale, NJ: Lawrence Erlbaum.
Gollin, A. E. (1985). *Newspapers in American news habits: A comparative assessment.* New York: Newspaper Advertising Bureau.
Gollin, A. E., & Salisbury, P. A. (1980). Three ways of assessing newspaper readership demographics. *Newspaper Research Journal, 1*(3), 27.
Newspaper Advertising Bureau. (1978). *The daily diet of news: Patterns of exposure to news in the mass media, 1978.* New York: Author.
Newspaper Advertising Bureau. (1978). *Young adults and the newspaper.* New York: Author.
Newspaper Advertising Bureau. (1980). *Children and newspapers: Changing patterns of readership and their effects, 1980.* New York: Author.
Newspaper Advertising Bureau. (1981). *Senior citizens and newspapers.* New York: Author.
Newspaper Advertising Bureau. (1984). *Changing lifestyles and newspaper reading: An exploratory panel study of younger adults.* New York: Author.
Rarick, G. R., & Lemert, J. B. (1986). Subscriber behavior and attitudes in response to PM—AM conversion. *Newspaper Research Journal, 7*(2), 11.
Salisbury, P. A. (1981). Older adults as older readers: Newspaper readership after age 65. *Newspaper Research Journal, 3*(1), 38.
Stamm, K. R. (1985). *Newspaper use and community ties: Toward a dynamic theory.* Norwood, NJ: Ablex.
Stone, G. C. (1986). No rest-in-peace for readers after PM's demise. *Newspaper Research Journal, 8*: 1-13.
Stone, G., & Windhauser, J. (1983). Young adults' content preferences based on morning vs. evening reading time. *Newspaper Research Journal, 4*(2), 9.

Demographics and Psychographics

Bogart, L. (1981). *Press and public: Who reads what, when, where, and why in American newspapers.* Hillsdale, NJ: Lawrence Erlbaum.
Einsiedel, E. F., & Tully, H. A. (1981). Newspaper use by working and non-working women. *Newspaper Research Journal, 2*(4), 69.

Friedman, B. J. (1985, May). Young blacks' readership higher than that of white counterparts. *Presstime,* p. 50.

Gollin, A. E. (1985). *Newspapers in American news habits: A comparative assessment.* New York: Newspaper Advertising Bureau.

Jackson, M. M. (1978, May 24). A comparison of newspaper use by lower-income and middle- and upper-income blacks. *ANPA News Research Report No. 11.*

Johnson, C., & Gross, L. (1985). Mass media use by women in decision-making positions. *Journalism Quarterly, 62,* 850-854.

Newspaper Advertising Bureau. (1978). *News sources and interests of blacks and whites.* New York: Author.

Newspaper Advertising Bureau. (1979). *Women and newspapers in the 1970's.* New York: Author.

Salisbury, P. (1981). Older adults as older readers: Newspaper readership after age 65. *Newspaper Research Journal, 3*(1), 38.

Schramm, W., & White, D. M. (1947). Age, education, economic status: Factors in newspaper reading. *Journalism Quarterly, 26,* 149-159.

Tipton, L. (1978, July 12). ANPA Newspaper Readership Studies. *ANPA News Research Report No. 13.*

Weaver, D. H., & Mauro, J. B. (1978). Newspaper readership patterns. *Journalism Quarterly, 55,* 84-91, 134.

Winter, J. P., & DeGeorge, W. F. (1980). Characteristics of newspaper coupon clippers. *Newspaper Research Journal, 2*(1), 29.

Beyond Raw Demographics

Becker, L. B., Collins, E. L., & Fruit, J. W. (1980, May 23). Personal motivations and newspaper readership. *ANPA News Research Report No. 26.*

Bryant, B. E., Currier, F. P., & Morrison, A. J. (1976). Relating life style factors of person to his choice of a newspaper. *Journalism Quarterly, 53,* 74-79.

Burgoon, J. K., & Burgoon, M. (1981). The functions of the daily newspaper. *Newspaper Research Journal, 2*(4), 29.

Einsiedel, E. F., & Kang, N. (1983). Civic attitudes among non-readers and non-subscribers. *Newspaper Research Journal, 4*(4), 37.

Jackson, K. M. (1982). Local community orientations of suburban newspaper subscribers. *Newspaper Research Journal, 3*(3), 52.

Kebbel, G. (1985). Strength of political activity in predicting newspaper use. *Newspaper Research Journal, 6*(2), 1.

Kline, F. G. (1971). Media time budgeting as a function of demographics and life style. *Journalism Quarterly, 48,* 211-221.

Larkin, E. F., Grotta, G. L., & Stout, P. (1977, April 8). The 21-34 year old market and the daily newspaper. *ANPA News Research Report No. 1.*

Mauro, J. B., & Weaver, D. H. (1977, July 22). Patterns of newspaper readership. *ANPA News Research Report No. 4.*

McCombs, M. (1983). Newspapers and the civic culture. *Newspaper Research Journal, 4*(4), 5.

McCombs, M., & Poindexter, P. (1983). The duty to keep informed: News exposure and civic obligation. *Journal of Communication, 33*(2), 88-96.

McLeod, J. M., & Choe, S. Y. (1978, March 14). An analysis of five factors affecting newspaper circulation. *ANPA News Research Report No. 10.*

Meyer, P. (1982, June 18). Psychographics made simple. *ANPA News Research Report No. 34.*

Newspaper Research Journal. [Special Edition]. (1983). *4*(4).

Olsen, O. (1983). Measuring civic attitudes: Replications and extensions. *Newspaper Research Journal, 4*(4), 19.

Poindexter, P. M. (1978, January 5). Non-readers: Why they don't read. *ANPA News Research Report No. 9.*

Schwartz, S. H., Moore, R. L., & Krekel, T. H. (1979). Life style and the daily paper: A psychographic profile of Midwestern readers. *Newspaper Research Journal, 1*(1), 9.

Schweitzer, J. C. (1977, December 2). Life style and readership. *ANPA News Research Report No. 8.*

Shaw, E. F. (1978, June 9). Newspaper reading in small towns. *ANPA News Research Report No. 12.*

Smith, H. H., III. (1986). Newspaper readership as a determinant of political knowledge and activity. *Newspaper Research Journal, 7*(2), 47.

Stamm, K. R., & Fortini-Campbell, L. (1981, October 30). Community ties and newspaper use. *ANPA News Research Report No. 33.*

Stephens, L. F. (1978, December 20). The influence of community attachment on newspaper reading habits. *ANPA News Research Report No. 17.*

Stevenson, R. L. (1979, March 9). Newspaper readership and community ties. *ANPA News Research Report No. 18.*

Stone, G. C. (1977). Community commitment: A predictive theory of daily newspaper circulation. *Journalism Quarterly, 54,* 509-514.

Stone, G. C. (1978, September 22). Using community characteristics to predict newspaper circulation. *ANPA News Research Report No. 14.*

Weaver, D., & Fielder, V. D. (1983). Civic attitudes and newspaper readership in Chicago. *Newspaper Research Journal, 4*(4), 11.

Westley, B., & Severin, W. H. (1964). A profile of the daily newspaper non-reader. *Journalism Quarterly, 41,* 45-50.

Application With Young Readers

Yankelovich, Skelly, and White, Inc. (1976, May). *Young people and newspapers: An exploratory study.* (Prepared for the Harte-Hanks Newspapers, Inc.)

6

AUDIENCE EFFECTS

The probable effect of newspapers on their audiences is presented through application of several modern communication theories and the theories' research findings that pertain most to the newspaper industry.

The final aspect of what research tells us about newspapers deals with the product's effect on audiences. This area rivals in quantity that of any other aspect of newspaper research. In addition, audience-effects concepts are more far-reaching: they are broader precepts about public use of the mass media generally and newspapers in particular. Since *use* is the key to this area of investigation, beginning with some cautions about how use has been measured will be beneficial.

NEWSPAPER "USE" MEASUREMENTS

How do researchers measure the extent of an audience's newspaper use? Obviously, the more leniently *use* is defined, the more use will be measured. For instance, if audience members are asked, "Do you read a daily newspaper?" they are likely to say yes since some individuals may interpret the question as, "Have you ever read a daily newspaper?" and answering it positively is a prosocial response. Larkin and Hecht's study (1979) of Oklahoma newspaper markets reported 91% of respondents surveyed "regularly read a newspaper." Since a Newspaper Advertising Bureau study (1978) reported "yesterday" readership at 69% nationwide the same year, either the Larkin question measuring newspaper use was amiss or the more rural Oklahoma respondents were more frequent newspaper readers. Considering the 22% difference in findings, both mitigating factors are likely to have been occurring.

These, from most lenient to most strict, are the frequently employed newspaper-use measures: (1) Do you read a daily newspaper occasionally; (2) do you usually read a daily newspaper; (3) how many days a week do you usually read a daily newspaper; (4) did you read a daily newspaper yesterday? Because it is used so often, "yesterday" readership has become the industry's standard newspaper use measure. However, Soley and Reid (1986) report the two-interview read-yesterday technique is necessary to estimate cumulative audiences for newspaper advertising.

Two-issue cume data—perhaps the most strict use measures—are compiled by asking the same respondent on two occasions if the newspaper was read yesterday. The problem with this method is its expense and newness. There are few previous studies to which findings can be compared.

Newspaper use measurement would be improved if standardization were sought, and if use measures were based on an index of use established by combining answers to several questions now being asked most frequently. This combination of questions might be employed:

(1) Do you usually read a daily newspaper?
(2) About how many days a week do you usually read a newspaper: one or two, three or four, five or more?
(3) Do you subscribe to a daily newspaper?
(4) Did you read a daily newspaper yesterday?
(5) When you read a daily newspaper, about how many minutes do you spend reading it?

The final question should be dichotomized to less than 15 minutes versus 15 minutes or more. These, and other questions (Stone & Wetherington, 1979), have been used successfully to establish a scale of personal commitment to newspaper reading. The more sophisticated index approach, if successfully verified, could provide a standardized measure of newspaper use. The industrywide measure would be extremely helpful in assessing the several modern theories of mass media use for which there is so much conflicting evidence.

There are four modern mass media theories that best assess newspaper audience effects: uses and gratifications, diffusion, knowledge gap, and agenda setting. Each is at least partially flawed, but each continues to add understanding to how newspapers are used by their publics.

USES AND GRATIFICATIONS

Initiated in the late 1950s, there have been several resurgences of interest in this approach to mass communication in the decades since (see references). The theory is simple and includes these basic tenets:

(1) People select from the wide range of media offerings those content items that interest them most.
(2) Selection of media messages is based on which content provides the most pleasure or reward. Such gratification can be either immediate or delayed.

(3) While the choice of content is an individual decision, general content preferences can be predicted by an audience member's socioeconomic status.

The "pleasure or reward" aspect here is not a reference to entertainment content alone, although entertainment is certainly an element of uses and gratifications. But while reading the comics is assumed to be an immediate gratification and entertainment reward, reading advice columns is thought to provide both immediate pleasure through the vicarious perusal of others' problems and some delayed reward through the lessons an individual may learn for use in his or her own life. Similarly, reading news about an arrest or murder is considered more the immediate, vicarious reward and reading news analyses or stories about government policy is considered more delayed reward. The "delayed" aspect of these reports is that information gleaned might be used in later conversations with friends or might help an individual make a future voting decision.

Research has confirmed that people in lower socioeconomic audience strata rely more heavily on entertainment and immediate gratification media content. People in higher socioeconomic strata are more likely to use delayed reward content. Both of these research findings are gross generalizations, but they have received consistent support over time.

Flaws in this theory of media use are legion, primarily because the theory is so encompassing. Difficulties arise in determining which media content items belong in the immediate versus the delayed reward categories. People's reports of their media use gratification are overlapping: some reward elements are entertainment; some are informational. Sometimes it isn't clear why audiences associate a particular hard news content item with other newspaper articles journalists may consider entertainment. Also, the socioeconomic divisions don't consistently predict content preferences in the expected manner.

The theory presents one major challenge for the newspaper industry in particular. Research has shown that people in the lowest socioeconomic stratum don't rely heavily on newspapers. Newspapers are primarily an information medium that appeals to the two-thirds of the population in the middle and higher socioeconomic strata. The theory suggests newspapers will have little appeal for the lowest third of the mass audience who are not now reading newspapers.

Regardless of its flaws, the theory does have face validity.

People will not attend to media messages that have no perceived interest value for them. They will choose among media content offerings those items they deem valuable, even if that value is only momentary enjoyment.

The single most significant aspect of uses and gratifications theory is its emphasis on the importance of the individual. Instead of viewing individuals as malleable pawns manipulated by the mass media, individuals are seen as having total control of their media use decisions. This theory says individuals will choose among the wide variety of media and messages those that offer them some recognizable value. The theory explains why some individuals will perpetually be among newspaper nonreaders, why most newspaper readers skip articles, why it's necessary to remind readers of what happened before in a continuing story, why news rack sales increase on days a dramatic picture tops page one, and why dropping a feature that gets little general readership may still result in some noticeable complaints and cancellations. Uses and gratifications is called a "weak media" theory because it assumes the media have little control over audience effects. Instead the theory attributes most power to individuals who will choose whether they will attend to the message.

While the most basic tenets of the theory must be accepted, the real problem for the newspaper industry is in practical application of the theory. Work is progressing in this area, but it has not yet provided direction for marketing or news-editorial content decisions.

INFORMATION DIFFUSION

The U.S. Department of Agriculture began diffusion studies with its 1920s investigation of farmers' adoption of hybrid seed corn (Rogers, 1962). These early studies sought to determine the process by which groups of people learn about and accept new inventions or new ideas. Communication was identified as one of the first steps in the diffusion process, and the mass media were found to be an influential part of communicating ideas to the public. Much has been learned about the effects of mass media—and the part played by newspapers in particular—from hundreds of research studies since the 1930s. Here are a few outcomes that pertain to the way people use newspapers for new ideas.

(1) There is a diffusion curve, or a flow in the way messages are received. While all the mass media may disseminate a message at nearly the same time, the audience doesn't receive it at the same time or in the same manner. Some will be direct receivers, others will be indirect, and some audience members won't get the message at all.

(2) The speed at which messages come through to audience members depends on individuals' socioeconomic status, since status relates to media use. People who can't read, for instance, may not learn of a

welfare policy change very quickly, although that information may be personally valuable.

(3) Different messages are received at different speeds. Almost everyone in the population will have learned details of a presidential assassination attempt within hours, depending on the time of day it occurs. The majority of the population, however, may require months to identify correctly which military faction in a foreign civil war is receiving U.S. aid.

(4) Most people first learn about a crisis by word of mouth. Depending on time of day, the broadcast media may be the next source of knowledge about a crisis. Newspapers are often last, but they are relied upon as the most thorough source of daily information. In noncrisis situations, the nature of the issue will suggest which mass medium will be remembered as the first to provide information.

Diffusion is another "weak media" theory, since it suggests quite a lengthy and involved process through which information gets to the individual. During much of this process as well, the individual decides whether attention will be paid the mass media. However, this theory attributes power to the mass media by acknowledging people will turn to them for needed information.

Flaws in the theory are plentiful. First, while it's clear crisis topics will be rapidly diffused through the population, it has been difficult to estimate the speed of diffusion for specific content topics. Second, an individual's personal utility for knowing some specific piece of information is likely to have more influence on that individual's media use than the person's socioeconomic status. Third, there is no distinct pattern of which medium people will turn to; it varies with topic type, topic importance, and time of day of news breaks, among other possible influences. Fourth, diffusion studies have devoted more attention to the spread of information about "innovations" than about information. We know more about the spread and acceptance of new products and new ways of doing things than we do about how "news" or general information is diffused through a mass audience. Finally, methodological inconsistencies associated with information diffusion studies have hampered the development of a comprehensive theory.

But, for news and general information, some of the basic tenets of the theory are important to the newspaper industry:

Information disseminated by newsapers does *not* reach the audience in a consistent or predictable manner. While crisis information spreads rapidly, less critical information may take months or years to be registered by the majority audience members. The audience, however, does rely on newspapers to provide depth reports on major breaking news stories.

As with other theories with broad implications, day-to-day applications of information diffusion theory are limited. Writers and editors should be aware of the probable flow of information they provide audiences, but the theory is not likely to alter their practice of gathering or processing the news.

KNOWLEDGE GAP CONSIDERATIONS

A relatively new area of audience efforts theory deals with the knowledge gap hypothesis. The basic elements of this media use theory are:

(1) Audiences can be divided into two types based on socioeconomic status. Those in the lower strata are disadvantaged in their media use abilities—for a variety of reasons—and rely more on the broadcast media for entertainment. Those in the higher strata rely on print media for information.
(2) Those in the upper socioeconomic strata are the media rich. They have access to more information and make better use of the mass media generally. They are more knowledgeable than the media poor; hence the "knowledge gap" is between the two socioeconomic groups.
(3) As the flow of information increases—due to the addition of media outlets such as cable television or the proliferation of magazines—the media rich will use the new channels for even greater information gain. The knowledge gap between the two groups will increase with the possible outcome of an even greater social-political distance between the two groups.

The theory is a "powerful media" theory, since it assumes processing information from the mass media increases knowledge and has far-reaching effects on society. The theory singles out print media as the more powerful influence, since newspapers, magazines, and books are seen as information providers while the broadcast media are viewed as entertainment providers. In fact, the research on knowledge gap indicates the media poor spend more time per day with television than do the media rich, but most of the additional time is spent viewing purely entertainment content. The theory offers a frightening view of audience effects, since it suggests further societal and political division. With increased information flow, the knowledge gap will grow and the media rich will become a more powerful elite.

Implications for newspapers are not as consequential as those for society. Already under way is specialization in reporting, larger newsholes due to more published pages and increased attention to science, new technology, health, and similar topics. The assumption here is that as more information is carried in newspapers, those who read newspapers faithfully will surge ahead in knowledge. Whether less faithful readers will gain or lose ground is not known. Additionally, we don't know if this more comprehensive coverage is linked to the loss in readership newspapers have experienced during the past 15 years. The theory may suggest former readers who couldn't cope with the increase in information became nonreaders.

It is not yet clear if *USA Today's* approach to coverage—shorter articles on a wider variety of topics—will be adopted by more of the newspaper industry. If a trend to shorter articles does develop, it isn't clear what effect that might have on audiences from a knowledge gap standpoint. At this writing, *USA Today's* readers are more upscale than most daily newspaper audiences, so the paper's new content strategy was not intended to appeal to lower socioeconomic status groups.

Knowledge gap theory has undergone significant alteration since it was offered in the early 1970s. In the first place, an audience member's education and perceived need for specific information has a greater effect on media attention and knowledge gain than socioeconomic status alone. Second, there is a "ceiling" effect: a point at which increased information results in little knowledge gain by the media rich, but may result in gains by the media poor (the knowledge gap *narrows*). Third, a person's previous knowledge on a topic has an inverse effect on knowledge gain: The higher the initial knowledge level, the less gain takes place. Fourth, the more conflict is associated with an issue, the less knowledge gap pertains since audience members will be drawn equally to a high-conflict topic. Finally, interpersonal communication—particularly on an issue that is highly relevant to the audience member—can counteract the individual's lack of print media use: The media poor can gain the knowledge they need without relying on the mass media.

The newspaper industry's readership loss since the 1970s may best be explained by knowledge gap theory. While the theory currently offers no suggestion for rebuilding reader bases, its implications are:

> Newspapers should consider possible content improvements which might appeal more to the media poor segments of society not now relying on print media for information. If gains could be made in the less-frequent or

nonreader strata without compromising journalistic quality, the audience base for newspapers might increase.

AGENDA-SETTING FUNCTION

The newest broad theory of audience effects is called agenda setting. Its strength lies in its major, irrefutable precepts:

The media can't tell audience members what to think (they aren't very successful persuaders), but the media do tell audience members what to think about. Media content sets people's personal agenda of what is important.

Agenda setting is a powerful media theory because it declares at any given time people possess a set of issues they can report as being both important to them personally and important to others (members of their community, state, or the nation). For all practical purposes, the issues people report as significant match the issues that have appeared prominently in the mass media. Those issues people name as most important are the ones likely to have received most extensive coverage in the mass media. Additionally, the research confirms issues reported in the media show up on the public agenda *later*. This last finding means the mass media set the public agenda rather than the other way around.

While the three other communication theories suggest the mass media have a difficult time penetrating audience defenses, or audience indifference, agenda setting asserts the messages—at least the important ones—are getting through. The process is less one of hitting a target with a bullet; it is more a process of flouridating water. People often are not aware they have ingrained mass media messages. Yet the research has shown people receive even a political candidate's main platform points during an election campaign and may have determined how to vote based on the acceptance of the reported campaign rhetoric.

Since its inception, the theory has generated considerable debate about exactly how the process works. Among questions critics raise are: (1) how long does it take an issue to be registered on the public agenda; (2) how long will an issue remain on the public agenda; (3) is the agenda set by local or national media; (4) is the agenda set by all mass media in concert or by a single medium; (5) do people act on the agenda items they have ingrained, and if so, under what circumstances; (6) to what extent does the type of issue or its importance determine whether it appears on the public agenda; (7) what audience characteristics determine if an issue will appear on the agenda of subgroups or individuals.

A few practical implications have emerged from the agenda-setting research. For instance, crisis issues such as the U.S. bombing of Libya in 1986 are likely to appear almost immediately on the public agenda; but noncrisis issues such as raising funds for America's homeless will reach the public agenda, if at all, only after extensive coverage. The theory also indicates some issues may receive too much attention too early. For instance, presidential campaigns dominate the mass media agenda beginning in the early spring of election years but don't register on the public agenda until late summer, usually during the major party conventions. These considerations will be more useful to agency public relations practitioners, or others seeking to influence public opinion, than to newspaper managers. Still, there are implications for news coverage of coming or continuing events.

But the theory has more value to the newspaper industry as reinforcement than as a guide for content or marketing decisions. It provides some satisfaction that informing the public is being achieved. Since news values dictate a topic will receive coverage as long as it is worthy of attention, the journalistic process need not change. But editors might be more sensitive to providing complete coverage to an important issue and less concerned about overplaying an issue that deserves public attention. Editors should be reassured that continuing series of news stories coupled with analyses and editorial page treatment are having the desired information effect and retaining readers, if such extensive coverage was ever doubted. The theory also raises the issue of responsibility to emphasize what is newsworthy; to give more prominent play to the most important aspects of a story and to downplay the trivial aspects.

While the agenda-setting function theory has its flaws, as do the other theories presented, the evidence an agenda-setting effect takes place among audiences is well documented by the research. It has both face validity and empirical validation.

COMMUNICATION THEORIES ASSESSED

These four mass media theories are offered as the most definitive guides to how audiences receive media messages. It is apparent none of them provides the kind of definitive findings the newspaper industry can use on a day-to-day basis for decision making. Since most of the theories are still in developmental stages, there is some promise more practical guidelines for newspaper managers will emerge. However, even if the research remains disappointing in that respect, the theories provide a worthwhile view of what may be happening when newspapers meet their audiences. Knowing how a message may affect newspaper readers should influence the way it is produced and disseminated by those responsible for the process.

REFERENCES

Newspaper "Use" Measurements

Larkin, E. F., & Hecht, T. L. (1979, April). Research assistance for the non-metro newspaper. *Newspaper Research Journal* [Prototype]: 62.

Newspaper Advertising Bureau. (1978). *The daily diet of news: Patterns of exposure to news in the mass media* (pp. 2-4). New York: Author.

Soley, L. C., & Reid, L. N. (1985). What audience data do newspapers provide advertisers? *Newspaper Research Journal, 6*(4), 1.

Stone, G. C., & Wetherington, R. V., Jr. (1979). Confirming the newspaper reading habit. *Journalism Quarterly, 56*, 554-561, 566.

Uses and Gratifications

Abrams, M. E., Kaul, A. J., & Ma, C. (1979). Social class and perceived utility of newspaper advertising. *Newspaper Research Journal, 1*(1), 42.

Allen, C. T., & Weber, J. D. (1983). How presidential media use affects individuals' beliefs about constitution. *Journalism Quarterly, 60*, 98-105.

Becker, L. B. (1975). Two tests of media gratifications: Watergate and the 1974 election. *Journalism Quarterly, 53*, 28-33, 87.

Becker, L. B., & Dunwoody, S. (1982). Media use, public affairs knowledge and voting in a local election. *Journalism Quarterly, 59*, 212-218.

Blumler, J. G., & Katz, E. (1974). *The uses of mass communications: Current perspectives on gratifications research.* Newbury Park, CA: Sage.

Burgoon, M., Burgoon, J. K., & Burch, S. A. (1981). Effects of editorial and production practices on satisfaction with the use of local daily newspapers. *Newspaper Research Journal, 2*(4), 77.

Conway, M. M., Stevens, A. J., & Smith, R. G. (1985). The relation between media use and children's civic awareness. *Journalism Quarterly, 52*, 531-538.

Einsiedel, E. F., & Tully, H. A. (1981). Newspaper use by working and non-working women. *Newspaper Research Journal, 2*(4), 69.

Fedler, F., Smith, R. F., & Counts, T. (1985). Voter uses and perceptions of editorial endorsements. *Newspaper Research Journal, 6*,(4), 19.

Johnson, C., & Gross, L. (1985). Mass media use by women in decision-making positions. *Journalism Quarterly, 62*, 850-854.

Kebbel, G. (1985). Strength of political activity in predicting newspaper use. *Newspaper Research Journal, 6*(2), 1.

Lain, L. B. (1985). More evidence on the needs of readers. *Newspaper Research Journal, 6*(4), 1.

McDonald, D. G., & Glynn, C. J. (1984). The stability of media gratification. *Journalism Quarterly, 61,* 542-549, 741.

Newspaper Research Journal [Special Issue]. (1983). *4*(4).

Rarick, G. R., & Lemert, J. B. (1986). Subscriber behavior and attitudes in response to PM-AM conversion. *Newspaper Research Journal, 7*(2), 11.

Schramm, W. (1949). The nature of news. *Journalism Quarterly, 26,* 259-269.

Singletary, M. W. (1985). Reliability of immediate reward and delayed reward categories. *Journalism Quarterly, 62,* 116-120.

Stone, G. C., & Trotter, E. P. (1979, April). Are suburbanites getting their news free in "Shoppers"? *Newspaper Research Journal* [Prototype]: 31.

Stroman, C. A., & Seltzer, R. (1985). Media use and perceptions of crime. *Journalism Quarterly, 62,* 340-345.

Towers, W. M. (1985). Weekday and Sunday readership seen through uses and gratifications. *Newspaper Research Journal, 6*(3), 20.

Weber, L. J., & Fleming, D. B. (1983). Media use and student knowledge of current events. *Journalism Quarterly, 60,* 356-358.

Weiss, R. J., & Stamm, K. R. (1982). How specific news interests are related to stages of settling in a community. *Newspaper Research Journal, 3*(3), 60.

Whitney, D. C., & Goldman, S. B. (1985). Media use and time of vote decision: A study of the 1980 presidential election. *Communication Research, 12,* 511.

Information Diffusion

Adams, R. C. (1981). Newspaper and television as news information media. *Journalism Quarterly, 58,* 627-629.

Atkin, C., Burgoon, J., & Burgoon, M. (1983). How journalists perceive the reading audience. *Newspaper Research Journal, 4,*(2), 51.

Bantz, C. R., Petronio, S. G., & Rarick, D. L. (1983). News diffusion after the Reagan shooting. *Quarterly Journal of Speech, 59,* 317-327.

Burgoon, J. K., Bernstein, J. M., & Burgoon, M. (1983). Public and journalist perceptions of newspaper functions. *Newspaper Research Journal, 5*(1), 77.

Carrocci, N. M. (1985). Diffusion of information about cyanide-laced Tylenol. *Journalism Quarterly, 62,* 630-633.

Fielder, V. D., & Weaver, D. H. (1982). Public opinion on investigative reporting. *Newspaper Research Journal, 3*(2), 54.

Fine, G. A. (1975). Recall of information about diffusion of major news event. *Journalism Quarterly, 52,* 751-755.

Funkhouser, G. R., & McCombs, M. E. (1971). The rise and fall of news diffusion. *Public Opinion Quarterly, 35,* 107-113.

Gantz, W., & Trenholm, S. (1979). Why people pass on news: Motivation for diffusion. *Journalism Quarterly, 56,* 365-370.

Gantz, W., Trenholm, S., & Pittman, M. (1976). The impact of salience and altruism on diffusion of news. *Journalism Quarterly, 53,* 727-732.

Haroldson, E. O., & Harvey, K. (1979). The diffusion of "shocking" good news. *Journalism Quarterly, 56,* 771-775.

Hicks, R. G. (1981) How much news is enough?" *Newspaper Research Journal, 2*(2), 58.

Jeffres, L. W., & Quarles, R. (1983). A panel study on news diffusion. *Journalism Quarterly, 60,* 722-725.

Katz, E., Adoni, H., & Parness, P. (1977). Remembering the news: What the picture adds to recall. *Journalism Quarterly, 54,* 231-239.

Ledingham, J. A., & Masel-Walters, L. (1985). Written on the wind: The media and Hurricane Alicia. *Newspaper Research Journal, 6*(2), 50.

Luttbeg, N. R. (1983). News consensus: Do U.S. newspapers mirror society's happenings? *Journalism Quarterly, 60*(3), 484-488, 578.

Ogan, C. L., & Lafky, S. A. (1983). 1981's most important events as seen by reporters, editors, wire services and media consumers. *Newspaper Research Journal, 5*(1), 63.

Quarles, R., Jeffres, L. W., Sanchez-Ilundain, C., & Neuwirth, K. (1983). News diffusion of assassination attempts of President Reagan and Pope John Paul II. *Journal of Broadcasting, 27,* 387-395.

Riffe, D., & Belbase, S. (1983). Decision-maker views on foreign news. *Newspaper Research Journal, 4*(3), 17.

Robinson, J. P. (1972). Mass communication and information diffusion. In F. G. Kline & P. J. Tichenor (Eds.), *Current perspectives in mass communication research.* Newbury Park, CA: Sage.

Rogers, E. M., & Shoemaker, F. F. (1971). *Communication of innovations: A cross-cultural approach.* New York: Free Press.

Schwartz, D. A. (1973). How fast does news travel? *Public Opinion Quarterly, 37,* 625-627.

Steinfatt, T., Gantz, W., Seibold, D. R., & Miller, L. D. (1973). News diffusion of the George Wallace shooting: The apparent lack of interpersonal communication as an artifact of delayed measurement. *Quarterly Journal of Speech, 59,* 401-412.

Toggerson, S. K. (1981). Media coverage and information-seeking behavior. *Journalism Quarterly, 58,* 89-93.

Wilkins, L. (1985). Television and newspaper coverage of a blizzard: Is the message helplessness? *Newspaper Research Journal, 6*(4), 51.

Knowledge Gap Considerations

Dervin, B. (1980). Communication gaps and inequities: Moving toward a reconceptualization. In B. Dervin & M. J. Voight (Eds.), *Progress in Communication Sciences* (Vol. 2, pp. 73-112. Norwood, NJ: Ablex.

Donohue, G. A., Tichenor, P. J., & Olien, C. N. (1973). Mass media functions, knowledge gap: A hypothesis reconsidered. *Communication Research, 2,* 10-23.

Donohue, G. A., Tichenor, P. J., & Olien, C. N. (1973). Mass media functions, knowledge and social control. *Journalism Quarterly, 50,* 652-659.

Ettema, J. S., & Kline, F. G. (1977). Deficits, differences and ceilings: Contingent conditions for understanding the knowledge gap. *Communication Research, 4,* 179-202.

Gandy, O. H., Jr., & El Waylly, M. (1985). The knowledge gap and foreign affairs: The Palestinian-Israeli conflict. *Journalism Quarterly, 62,* 777-783.

Gaziano, C. (1983. The knowledge gap: An analytical review of media effects. *Communication Reseach, 10,* 477-486.

Gaziano, C. (1984). Neighborhood newspapers, citizen groups and public affairs knowledge gaps. *Journalism Quarterly, 61,* 556-566.

Genova, B., & Greenberg, B. (1979). Interest in news and the knowledge gap. *Public Opinion Quarterly, 43,* 79-91.

Lovrich, N. P., Jr., & Pierce J. C. (1984). "Knowledge gap" phenomena: Effect of situation-specific and transsituational factors. *Communication Research, 11,* 415-434.

Olien, C. N., Donohue, G. A., & Tichenor, P. J. (1978). Community structure and media use. *Journalism Quarterly, 55,* 445-455.

Olien, C. N., Donohue, G. A., & Tichenor, P. J. (1983). Structure, communication and social power: Evolution of the knowledge gap hypothesis. In E. Wartella & D. C. Whitney (Eds.), *Mass Communication Yearbook* (Vol. 4). Newbury Park, CA: Sage.

Roberts, D. F., & Bachen, C. (1981). Mass communication effects. *Annual Review of Psychology, 32,* 307-356.

Robinson, J. P. (1967). World affairs information and mass media exposure. *Journalism Quarterly, 44,* 23-31.

Tichenor, P. J., Donohue, G. A., & Olien, C. N. (1970). Mass media flow and differential growth in knowledge. *Public Opinion Quarterly, 34,* 159.

Tichenor, P. J., Rodenkrichen, J., Olien, C., & Donohue, G. A. (1973). Community issues, conflict, and public affairs knowledge. In P. Clarke (Ed.), *New Models for Communication Research.* Newbury Park, CA: Sage.

Agenda-Setting Function

Atwater, T., Salwen, M. B., & Anderson, R. B. (1985). Interpersonal discussion as a potential barrier to agenda-setting. *Newspaper Research Journal, 6*(4), 37.

Atwater, T., Salwen, M. B., & Anderson, R. B. (1985). Media agenda-setting with environmental issues. *Journalism Quarterly, 62,* 393-397.

Benton, M., & Frazier, P. J. (1976). The agenda-setting function of the mass media at three levels of information holding. *Communication Research, 3,* 261-274.

Cook, F. L. et al. (1983) Media and agenda-setting: Effects on the public, interest group leaders, policy makers, and policy. *Public Opinion Quarterly, 47,* 16-35.

Culbertson, H. M. (1983, June). Three perspectives on American journalism. *Journalism Monographs, No. 83,* pp. 29-30.

Culbertson, H. M., & Stempel, G. H., III. (1984). Possible barriers to agenda setting in medical news. *Newspaper Research Journal, 5*(3), 53.

Downs, A. (1972). Up and down with ecology—The "Issue-Attention Cycle." *The Public Interest, 28,* 38-50.

Elder, C. (1972). *Participation in American politics: The dynamics of agenda-building.* Boston: Allyn & Bacon.

Erbring, L., Goldenberg, E. N., & Miller, A. H. (1980). Front-page news and real world cues. *American Journal of Political Science, 24,* 16-49.

Gandy, O. (1982). *Beyond agenda setting: Information subsidies and public policy.* Norwood, NJ: Ablex.

Gaziano, C. (1985). Neighborhood newspaper and neighborhood leaders: Influences on agenda setting and definitions of issues. *Communication Research, 12,* 568.

Gilberg, S., Eyal, C., McCombs, M., & Nicholas, D. (1980). The state of the Union Address and the press agenda. *Journalism Quarterly, 57,* 584-588.

Gormley, W. T. (1975). Newspaper agendas and political ethics. *Journalism Quarterly, 52,* 304-308.

Kaid, L. L., Hale, K., & Williams, J. A. (1977). Media agenda setting of a specific political event, *Journalism Quarterly, 54,* 584-587.

Kraus, S., & Davis, D. (1976). *The effects of mass communication on political behavior.* University Park: Pennsylvania State University Press.

McClure, R. D., & Paterson, T. E. (1978). Setting the political agenda: Print vs. network news. *Journal of Communication, 26,* 23-28.

McCombs, M. (1981). The agenda-setting approach. In D. D. Nimmo & K. R. Sanders (Eds.), *Handbook of political communication.* Newbury Park, CA: Sage.

McCombs, M., & Shaw, D. (1972). The agenda-setting function of the mass media. *Public Opinion Quarterly, 36,* 176-187.

McLeod, J. M., Becker, L. B., & Byrnes, J. E. (1974). Another look at the agenda-setting function of the press. *Communication Research, 1,* 131-166.

Shaw, D. L., & McCombs, M. E. (Eds.). (1977). *The emergence of American political issues: The agenda-setting function of the press.* St. Paul, MN: West.

Sohn, A. B. (1984). Newspaper agenda-setting and community expectations. *Journalism Quarterly, 61,* 892-897.

Stone, G., & McCombs, M. (1981). Tracing the time lag in agenda setting. *Journalism Quarterly, 58,* 51-55.

Weaver, D. (1982). Media agenda-setting and media manipulation. In D. C. Whitney & E. Wartella (Eds.), *Mass Communication Yearbook* (Vol. 3). Newbury Park, CA: Sage.

Weaver, D. (1984). Media agenda-setting and public opinion: Is there a link? In R. Bostrom (Ed.), *Communication Yearbook 9.* Newbury Park, CA: Sage.

Weaver, D., & Elliott, S. N. (1985). Who sets the agenda for the media? A study of local agenda-building. *Journalism Quarterly, 62,* 87-94.

Weaver, D., Graber, D., McCombs, M., & Eyal, C. H. (1981). *Media agenda-setting in a presidential election.* New York: Praeger.

Zucker, H. G. (1978). The variable nature of news media influence. In B. D. Ruben (Ed.), *Communication Yearbook* (Vol. 2). New Brunswick, NJ: Transaction Books.

NAME INDEX

SUBJECT INDEX

ABOUT THE AUTHOR

GERALD C. STONE is Professor of Journalism at Memphis State University, where he heads the graduate studies program and teaches journalism research and mass communication theory, as well as undergraduate newswriting and reporting courses. He is founding and current editor of *Newspaper Research Journal.* He has published articles in *Journalism Quarterly, Newspaper Research Journal, Journalism Educator, Feedback, Advertising Age, Nieman Reports, The Quill, Editor & Publisher, Computer Graphics World,* and *College Press Review.* He has authored communication yearbook articles, book chapters, and special research reports. Stone is co-author, with Michael Singletary, of a forthcoming textbook, *Communication Theory and Research Applications* (Ames, IA: Iowa State University Press).

NOTES